LAST KNOWN ALIVE

The Search for Sergeant First Class Donald L. Sparks

WIA, MIA, POW

Arlyn W. Perkey

Wisdom of Life Series

Learning Moments Press
Pittsburgh, PA

Last Known Alive:
The Search for Sergeant First Class Donald L. Sparks
WIA, MIA, POW

Published by Learning Moments Press
Pittsburgh, PA 15139
learningmomentspress.com

Copyright © 2019 by Arlyn Perkey
All rights reserved, including the right of reproduction
in whole or in part in any form.

ISBN-13: 978-0-9993638-3-6 (Print book)
ISBN13: 978-0-9993638-4-3 (eBook)

About the Covers

Front Cover: The series of photos from bottom to top represents the transition in Don's service. The picture of Don in his dress Army uniform was taken during Basic Training and is how he appeared when he left Iowa in 1969. The second photo represents Don's time in the bush as an infantryman and the search that continues for his remains as an unreturned POW. The third picture comes from a web site maintained by Don's company in a section titled "Unknown Men." We don't know who submitted the photo, but we are grateful. It is the only known photo of Don in Vietnam, and the last one we have of him. The background is a photo of my dress uniform. It is identical to the one Don is wearing in the first picture.

Back Cover: A picture of Donald L Sparks' name on the Vietnam Veterans Memorial Wall. The cross left of Don's name indicates he is missing action and unaccounted for.

BISAC Subject:
Biography & Autobiography/Military (BIO 008000)
Biography & Autobiography/Personal Memoir (BIO 026000)
History: Military: Vietnam (HIS 027120)

Onix audience Code:
01 General/Trade

Book Layout:
Mike Murray, pearhouse.com

Photography and Cover Layout:
Patrick L. Hoover and Mike Murray

This book is dedicated to individuals who, like Donald L. Sparks, served their country in Vietnam with the best of intentions.

TABLE OF CONTENTS

List of Maps 2

Glossary of Terms 3

Prologue 9

Chapter 1 | Expectations of Life and Death 15

Chapter 2 | I Have Myself Ready 23

Chapter 3 | Cherry in the Bush 33

Chapter 4 | An Eye for an Eye 47

Chapter 5 | Bait 53

Chapter 6 | Capture 69

Chapter 7 | Hospital 87

Chapter 8 | Into the Mountains 97

Chapter 9 | Letters 105

Chapter 10 | Re-Entering the World 121

Chapter 11 | Anguish 129

Epilogue | Remembering Don Sparks 141

Acknowledgments 147

Appendix 1 | Timeline of Events 149

Appendix 2 | Chains of Command 155

Appendix 3 | Key Military Grid Locations 158

LIST OF MAPS

MAP 1:   Ambush Sites along the Song Be (Visual Reference for Chapter 4, An Eye for an Eye and Chapter 5, Bait).

MAP 2:   Location of December 9, 1969 Ambush: Arlyn Perkey WIA (Visual Reference for Chapter 5, Bait).

MAP 3:   Location of Donald Sparks' Capture (Visual Reference for Chapter 6, Capture).

MAP 4:   Location of CK 120 Hospital (Visual Reference for Chapter 7, Hospital).

MAP 5:   Overview of Locations from Site of Capture to Unknown Location (Visual Reference for Chapters 6, Capture; Chapter 7, Hospital; Chapter 8, Into the Mountains).

MAP 6:   Location of Tien Lanh Village, Thon Bon Hamlets, Cau Chim Crossroads, and Jungle Camp (Visual Reference for Chapter 7, Hospital and Chapter 8, Into the Mountains).

MAP 7:   Proximity Map (Visual Reference for Chapter 9, Letters).

GLOSSARY OF TERMS

An	Village.
Boonies	Nickname for the field; not a Loading Zone or Fire Support Base.
Cau	Bridge.
CA	Combat Assault; This is a little bit of a misnomer most of these were just transporting troops from a fire support base (see FSB) to the field.
CC	Command and Control; helicopters that commanders flew in to direct ground troops.
CMD	Command.
CO	Commanding Officer.
Co	Company; normally included 100-125 people.
CP	Command Post; This unit consisted of the company radio operator, Battalion radio operator, Commanding Officer, Executive Officer, 1st Sergeant, Artillery officer, Artillery Radio Operator and from time to time another person or two. Mainly set up within the perimeter of two platoons and ran the whole show.
C-Rations	Canned meals also containing small packets of essentials.
Claymore	An antipersonnel mine.
Contact	Informal term referring to engagement with the enemy.
Contact Area	Place where we were engaged with the enemy.
Cobra	Aka Blue Max. a helicopter gunship with tremendous firepower.

DEROS	**D**ate of **E**xpected **R**eturn from **O**vers**S**eas. Most people had their DEROS firmly memorized and many inked it on their helmet cover.
DOD	Department of Defense.
DPAA	Defense POW/MIA Accounting Agency.
Dust off	Medevac helicopter, usually a Huey.
FSB	Fire Support Base, also referred to as an LZ or Landing Zone.
Field	Any time/place the company was off the fire support base.
Free Fire Zone	An area where South Vietnamese loyal to the government were not to be; if a Vietnamese was seen they were presumed to be enemy and could be fired on.
Grunt	Slang term used for an American infantry soldier.
Heavies	Full pack and gear.
Hooch	Slang term for a place to live, either a soldier's living quarters or a Vietnamese hut.
Hooched	Verb; usually two grunts who snapped their ponchos together to make a tent-like shelter they could stay out of the rain and sleep in.
Huey/Bird	Helicopter.
Humped	Slang for carried, also moved through the bush carrying full pack and gear; for example, I humped the machine gun and we humped all morning.
KIA	Killed in Action.
LIB	Light Infantry Brigade.
Log	Short for logistics; meaning supplied; Example; A log bird dropped c-rations and ammo. Means a helicopter brought in C Rations (food) and ammunition.
Log Day	Log days were when we were re-supplied in the field. Most times the helicopters could land and we were able to unload the supplies by hand.

Glossary of Terms

	However when the jungle did not allow this we got a "kick-out" which meant they just pushed the supplies out of the door of the chopper. "kick-outs" were never fun since this meant water would be put into large ammo containers. The water from these tasted really bad! Also we could not get new troops, i.e. Scout Dogs etc. Normal supplies were "C-rations", water, mail, ammo, and any small items like batteries or repair stuff. We were normally logged every 3 days when we were in the field.
LOH	Light Observation Helicopter; sometimes called "Snoopies."
LRRP	Slang for "ready to eat meals" that were associated with LRRP defined below. Later they were used by all infantry. Most grunts carried one meal of C-Rations and 1 meal of LRRP per day when we expected to be in the field before re-supply (usually 3 days).
LRRP	aka, "Lurps" Long Range Reconnaissance Patrol. These were teams of four to six soldiers inserted into the jungle by themselves. They would attempt to keep under cover and just watch enemy movement.
LZ	LZ Landing Zone We were working out of LZ Ellen (The Bait), LZ Jerri (Eye For An Eye).
M-16	Standard issue weapon for all personnel in Vietnam.
M-60	A light weight, 30 caliber machine gun that was commonly used during the Vietnam war. Typically one person in each squad carried the M-60 and another person carried extra ammunition.
M-79	A grenade launcher capable of firing a 40mm grenade or a "buckshot" round.
MIA	Missing in Action; a military term for a soldier who is missing but whose death cannot be confirmed

MOS	Military Occupational Specialty.
Nui	Mountain.
NVA	Acronym for "North Vietnamese Army," the name used by the United States and South Vietnam to refer to troops that come from North Vietnam to invade South Vietnam.
PAVN	Acronym for "Peoples Army of Vietnam" – This is how the North Vietnamese referred to themselves. They wanted to be recognized as the army of all Vietnamese with no distinction between north and south. They wanted re-unification.
Political Officer	Representative of the PAVN, whose job, according to Political Officer Captain Lam encompassed three objectives. The first is to drive a wedge between the people and their government—to make the people hate their government, and the Americans. Our second objective is to get people to join our (VC) armed forces. The third is to persuade them to increase their production of food, and give the increase to us. (Page 670, After Action Report).
POW	Prisoner of war. A soldier that has been taken captive by the enemy.
Rallier	Viet Cong defector.
RPG	Rocket propelled grenade. (aka B40) These were Chinese or Russian made weapons that are still being used today. Very effective and cheap weapon.
San Bay	Airfield.
Song	River.
Suoi	Stream.
The "World"	The United States; life back home.
Tinh	first order administrative division in Vietnam.
VC	Acronym for Viet Cong, the communist guerrilla forces in South Vietnam, National Liberation

Glossary of Terms

	Front. These troops were from South Vietnam, in contrast to NVA troops that moved south from North Vietnam. Many VC were killed in the Tet Offensive of 1968. These losses were replaced by NVA.
WIA	Wounded in Action.
Xa	Village.

PROLOGUE

AS A CHILD IN THE 1950'S, I played with toy guns and imagined myself as a hero like Roy Rogers, The Cisco Kid, and Wyatt Earp. My mind occasionally played Army, and I even visualized being wounded in battle. But I always survived. This make-believe world was in our rolling-hill cow pasture adjacent to my family's farmstead in Iowa. By the time I graduated from Iowa State University in 1968, my active imagination had been somewhat tempered. And, soon after graduation, I came face-to-face with the realities of war when I was drafted into the U.S. Army and sent to Vietnam.

When I was in Vietnam, I believed my country's motives for being there were honorable. We were helping the South Vietnamese resist invasion from North Vietnam so they could have a communist-free government. That was good for them and in turn good for America. I certainly never thought of myself as an occupier of their country. I never thought about how, to a Vietnamese, I must look like a soldier enforcing colonial rule for the French government. Vietnam had been occupied for generations, but I had neither studied nor thought much about the country's history. Unfortunately, neither had most of America, including American leaders for the preceding 35 years.

I never thought further back than the Gulf of Tonkin incident in the summer of 1964. While that so-called event was clearly a turning point for America's involvement, understanding of America's role goes back to the latter months of World War II. I was not aware of that history until I read two books that included information from Daniel Ellsberg's *Pentagon Papers.*[1]

Understanding the history of the Vietnam War, although vital, is far beyond the scope of this book. I don't focus on the decisions made by Presidents, Senators, Generals or anyone famous. This is the story of two young men at the other end of the power spectrum; one who survived the war and one who did not. One who had a very ordinary experience for an infantryman and one who had a very extraordinary experience. One who came home and enjoyed a productive life, and one whose remains are still in Vietnam.

At age 73, my perspective has changed somewhat. I still love America. I still believe in national defense and national interest. I would still serve if called. However, I no longer assume that every decision made for America is always in the best interest of our country. I am able to separate my love of country from my agreement or disagreement with what she does in every instance. I also accept that in this democracy we are still blessed that the ultimate responsibility for what we do as a nation rests with the people, including me. It is my responsibility to inform myself and then vote my convictions. I hope in some way, these two true stories contribute to readers' understanding of that tumultuous era and the price paid by those who gave their all.

In pondering the aftermath of the Vietnam War, a verse from a song written by Stevie Wonder and covered by Barbra Streisand in 1974, has played in my mind. "All In Love Is Fair" was popular before the Fall of Saigon, when it was becoming obvious what the outcome of the war was going to be. The lyrics of the verse follow:

> But all in war is so cold
> You either win or lose
> When all is put away
> The losing side I'll play.

Whether the loss of the war was inevitable is still debated as is who bears ultimate responsibility for the 58,318 names on the polished black granite Vietnam Memorial Wall. After 50 years, the loss is still

---

1 Michael Maclear, *The Ten Thousand Day War, Vietnam: 1945-1975,* London: Methuen, 1981, and Stanley Karnow, *VIETNAM: A History: The First Complete Account of Vietnam at War.* London: Penguin Books, 1983.

with many, and the question remains, with little good to show for it, what can we learn from this tragic episode in our history?

Donald L Sparks
Carroll, Iowa
BS Iowa State University 1968
Drafted into US Army 1968
Infantry - Vietnam 1969
WIA, MIA, POW
(not returned)

Arlyn W Perkey
Prairie City, Iowa
BS Iowa State University 1968
Drafted into Us Army 1968
Infantry – Vietnam 1969
WIA

SIMILAR CHOICES, DIFFERENT OUTCOMES

Like the rolling hills and roads through fields of corn and soybeans in Don's Iowa homeland, years have passed since his wounding and capture in Vietnam.

In high school, Don Sparks (no hat) and his brother Ron were active Future Farmers of America.
PHOTOGRAPH COURTESY OF THE SPARKS FAMILY

*The farm house Don departed in 1969 looks much as it did.
His younger brother, Russell, lives there now.*

*This is the farm where Calvin and Arloha Sparks raised livestock while
rearing their four children with love—instilling a sense of responsibility and
respect for others; values Don took to Vietnam.*

CHAPTER 1

EXPECTATIONS OF LIFE AND DEATH

I STARTED LIFE ON A FARM near the small town of Pella, Iowa. Each Fall, my father, Lynn, hooked his red Farnmall tractor to a green John Deere elevator with yellow steel wheels. One fall, when I was about six years old, I stood outside our front-yard gate and watched with fascination as Dad backed the tractor and elevator up a hill. Preoccupied, he manipulated the ungainly equipment toward the corn crib. At my feet was a kitten, just old enough to begin exploring its world, but not yet aware of potential dangers. Dad didn't see the unwary kitten wander into the path of a moving steel wheel. In an instant, the tiny body flopped around; then lay motionless. In that instant, I realized for the first time that living things die.

I cried and was mad at my dad for killing the kitty, but as was usual, he left it to my mother to handle my feelings. I don't remember her exact words, but she probably reassured me that Daddy didn't mean to hurt the kitten. It was an accident and accidents just happen.

Shortly after my 11th birthday, I learned my maternal grandfather had brain cancer. After surgery that left a sunken dip in his forehead, I figured out from his appearance and listening to adults talk that things were not going to end well. On March 3, 1957, he died. He was the first person that I really loved who died.

These two events formed my early expectations regarding death. Although many details were different, both losses had one detail in common. I knew what happened, where it happened, and how it happened. This is how I learned to process the loss of life. I had an expectation of understanding the circumstances of death. Having someone simply "be gone," without knowing what happened was not normal; it was a reality I found hard to accept. Yet that was exactly the reality for the family of Donald L. Sparks.

For 49 years, the expectation that the circumstances of a loved one's death can be known and mourned has been unfilled for Don's family. For 49 years, his sister Esta has yearned for some resolution; to know finally what happened to her older brother. "If Don's remains are recovered and returned to me," Esta says, "I would open the casket to see what is left of him. I don't care how little there is or what condition. I want to see for myself. If it is just a few bones and teeth, fine. I want to see the remains of my brother. In my opinion, visual proof is very important. For me, it will finally be closure. Don will be home with us where he belongs, and we will bury him next to his parents."

****

Don and I were both Iowa farm boys whose families lived about 114 miles apart. We met as freshman at Iowa State University where I had gone to study forestry and Don to study farm operations. I had planned to share a three-man room with two friends from my hometown. However, after a week, the two friends decided Iowa State was not for them and departed. They were replaced by students on the dorm-room waiting list. Never one to be pressured by punctuality, Don, from Carroll, Iowa, was on the list and assigned to join me and another freshman in Room 2335, Dodds House, Friley Hall.

Perhaps it was our shared farming background that helped us to find common ground and form a congenial relationship. I had already settled into the top bunk, and Don took the bed below me. I studied at the library until it closed at midnight. Don didn't share these nightly study habits, but never complained about my coming home late, taking a shower, and climbing into the overhead bunk. Maybe he was just glad he didn't have to be the one clambering around in the half dark.

Don was an interesting combination of quiet and fun loving. Although he was never loud, bellicose, or belligerent, his ornery smile revealed a personality that enjoyed a good laugh. He often had a sparkle in his eye that reflected his good nature and sense of humor. He liked people and enjoyed socializing; dedicating more time to it than I, the more serious one, did.

Don and I shared the shock of coming from small schools and discovering we were less prepared for the university environment than our fellow freshman who came from bigger schools. Although we had been accustomed to doing much better than most of our high school peers, at Iowa State we were no longer in the top performing academic group.

Being demoted from excellent to average took a toll on my self-esteem; something already in short supply at best. In classes, like English, Don and I struggled. Oh, we could spell and punctuate and diagram sentences, but were stunned to see others who understood theme-writing and supporting every statement with cold hard facts. We hadn't done that in our high schools, so when our first themes merited a D or an F, we had to pick ourselves off the floor. I describe my freshman English as an experience I crawled through on my hands and knees. Sometimes I think I passed because I always showed up for class, paid attention to the teacher, and conveyed the impression of caring and trying. Misery does love company, and Don and I were good company to each other.

Because of negative social experiences with a few high school peers, my self-esteem needed a boost, especially regarding acceptance. I needed assurance that others in my age group liked me. Donny was key in giving me that positive reinforcement. Probably, he never knew how much that mattered to me, because I never told him. At the time, I don't think I really understood it myself.

Although others called him Don, I called him Donny, perhaps in recognition of the ornery streak I saw in him. He never objected to the name. Decades later, his sister Esta told me that their mother also called him Donny, a nugget he had probably not wanted me to know and use as a tease.

Based on a recommendation from an older Iowa State student from my home town, I enrolled in Army ROTC. This could have led to my being an officer in the United States Army, but lacking self-confidence, I knew that being a leader and assertively telling others what to do was not for me. Besides, spending all that time polishing shoes and primping a uniform had little appeal. At the end of three weeks, I dropped out. Unlike me, Donny had the good sense to know the military wasn't for him without having to do a trial run. Not that our distaste for military life would matter in the years ahead.

The Gulf of Tonkin incident in the summer of 1964 set us on a collision course with events that neither of us actively chose to avoid. As the Vietnam War unfolded during our college years, we were not opposed to it. We didn't think of it as immoral and certainly didn't protest it. We were sons of what is now referred to as "The Greatest Generation." Although as farmers, our fathers were exempt from military service during World War II, they along with our mothers and most rural Iowans were staunchly patriotic and highly supportive and respectful of those who served. That sense of patriotism and duty was naturally ingrained in Donny and me. At least for me, I had no objection to the war. I just didn't like the idea of being yelled at or yelling at anyone else. I didn't want to be disciplined or be the disciplinarian.

Both of us graduated with Bachelor degrees from Iowa State in 1968. Like Dustin Hoffman's character Benjamin in *The Graduate*, I was a bit of a lost soul. Naively I let events take their natural course, allowing myself to be drafted instead of seeking an alternative form of military service. With my college education, I assumed I wouldn't be in the infantry. Besides, I loathed the idea of spending more time in the army than I absolutely had to. Unlike Benjamin in the movie, I did have a career I wanted to pursue. This line of thinking was a gross failure to understand what was happening around me.

Don tried to enlist in the Air Force, but he had waited too long to pursue that alternative. At the time, enlistments in the Air Force and Navy were common choices for those willing to serve, but not wanting to chance wading through the jungle and swamps of Vietnam. The option was so popular that enlistment quotas often filled quickly.

So, Don and I graduated; our naiveté putting us on paths to Vietnam as infantrymen in the Army. However, because Don and I lost contact after graduation, I didn't know he, too, had been sent to Vietnam. This discovery came in November 1983, when my wife at the time, brought me literature she had picked up at the Vietnam Veterans Memorial Wall. With shock, I saw the picture of my Iowa State college roommate on the front cover of a POW flyer. I looked at the picture again and again in disbelief. But the picture didn't disappear. There was no doubt. It was Donald "Donny" L. Sparks.

****

In 2014, thirty-one years after that shocking discovery, I felt a need to reach out to Don's family. I wanted to know if they had had contact with those in Don's company when he was captured. John Ealy, a mutual friend of Don's and mine, put me in touch with Don's sister Esta. Sadly, she had no first-hand information from the last Americans who saw Don before he went missing. I asked if she wanted me to contact the men who had been with him. She emphatically responded, yes. While the Department of Defense is charged with the task of recovering Don's remains if at all possible, they are not obligated to investigate how he became a POW.

Some might wonder, "What does it matter? He's dead; don't you get that? What difference does it make whether his remains are sent home after so many years have passed? Just move on. Just let it go." But we couldn't. Esta wanted to know; had a right to know. I needed to know. So, we embarked on a journey to discover the circumstances of Don's capture and time as a POW.

I confess to being somewhat motivated by survivor guilt. On December 9, 1969, I was gunshot with an AK-47. This "million-dollar-wound" was my ticket back home—alive and able to enjoy a good productive life. When I first learned of Don's POW status, I assumed it to be an odd incident, the result of a Landing Zone being overrun or a downed helicopter with Don being an injured survivor. When I learned his infantry unit had been ambushed, it sank in, "That could have been me. There but for the grace of God go I." I asked myself, "If that were me, would I want someone to learn what happened and tell my family and friends?" The answer was YES.

Don gave his all; everything he had expected of life. Even if he miraculously appeared alive tomorrow, he would be 72 years old, with no chance of regaining the normal life he should have had. Beyond his probable death, Don's sacrifice entailed whatever he endured in captivity. His valor is amplified, because his predicament was unknown for so long. He suffered alone without family and friends knowing of his plight. Except for an almost unbelievable series of events, his capture and survival as a prisoner of war would never have been revealed to the outside world. Call it fate or God's will, but the magnitude of his sacrifice is overwhelming.

To me, Don deserves the same respect and honor that we accord those who lost their lives storming the beaches of France on D-Day. True, the cause did not rise to the same level. Those soldiers who lost their lives in World War II truly fought for this country's freedom as well as the freedom of many other nations. The Vietnam War will not go down in history as a noble war to preserve the freedom of Americans. However, that is not Don Sparks' fault. Misguided decisions by government officials do not detract from the enormity of his sacrifice. It does not lessen the pain of his family and friends. He is certainly no less dead.

One of the greatest emotional burdens for a combat veteran is to have a comrade left behind. Thankfully, I never personally experienced that. But Don Sparks was left behind. He did not go to Vietnam and simply fall off the face of the earth. Those who loved him deserve to know what happened. Having given the full measure of patriotism, he deserves the respect and honor of his country. If possible, he should be laid to rest beside his parents. If that is not possible, then the least that can be done—the least that I can do—is, to the greatest extent possible, remove the burden of not knowing the circumstances of his death. I set out to accomplish that end. As a friend, a fellow grunt, and a fellow Vietnam Veteran, I owe Don that. And so, I committed to Esta, "I am going to do the best I can for Don."

****

Last Known Alive is a twofold story; a story constructed from my memories and from the research I have done into Don's ultimate fate. Throughout the book, I have interwoven my experiences as a soldier with those of Don's in order to convey what it was like to be an infantryman in Vietnam.

Chapter 1 21

To clarify and confirm memories of my experience, I reconnected with several of the men who had served in the same squad as I had. In my search for answers about the circumstances of Don's capture and the events that followed, I turned to on-line sources, telephone conversations with veterans from Don's company, and several of Don's childhood friends. Each of these sources added to the picture of my time and Don's in Vietnam. So, too, did Department of Defense interviews with former Vietnamese captors and caregivers who provided details about where Don was taken after he was captured, how he was treated, how he was regarded, and how he tried to escape.[2]

Through the interviews, conversations, and official records, I have tried to confirm as many facts as possible. However, after so many years, accounts of June 17, 1969 remain obscure. Records are incomplete and sometimes inaccurate. In fact, my investigations have led me to conclude that those writing the official reports incorrectly assumed that Don had died during the June 17 ambush. Key documents appear to be designed to convince those in authority that Don was dead. The intent was not malicious, but rather to "clear the books," of an inconvenient case. Those incorrect, unintentionally damaging words should not be allowed to stand as the last written record of Don Sparks' fate. To me that is a desecration. Before I pass from this earth, I want to see words on the virtual Vietnam Veterans Memorial Wall that reflect what we know about Don's being Wounded In Action, Missing In Action, and a Prisoner Of War who died on an unknown date in service to his country.

As I laid out events that happened to Don and me in Vietnam and events that happened during my research, four issues became apparent. One is the sequence of events and when information about those events came to light. In an effort to clarify this issue, I have included a timeline in Appendix 1.

A second issue is the number of people I mention, including those who served with me and with Don. During the Vietnam War, the

---

[2] The 1992/1993 Defense Authorization Act included a Section 1082. Disclosure of Information Concerning United States Personnel Classified as Prisoner of War or Missing in Action during the Vietnam Conflict. Post-war interviews with Vietnamese by Defense POW/MIA Accounting Agency personnel provided the core of what we know about Don's post-capture ordeal.

organization of companies, platoons, and squads was often in flux. The Chains of Command were fairly dynamic as officers and soldiers were wounded, killed, or completed their tour of duty. For officers, a typical 1-year tour of duty would include six out of twelve months in the field. For career officers having combat command experience was premium experience. For everyone to have a good opportunity, terms at desirable field commands were often limited. This made for frequent turnover. Also, many enlisted personnel managed to get jobs in the rear before their one-year tour was expired. Because this type of turnover affected the composition of Don's squad and mine, I have included three charts illustrating the Chain of Command and squad personnel during three key incidents. (See Appendix 2.)

Third, to make the location of various events easier to visualize, I have sketched seven maps of the areas I am referencing. In addition to these schematics, Appendix 3 contains military grid addresses that can be searched on Google Earth Pro to find key locations and view how they appear now. These might be of interest to those who want more detail regarding Don's various locations. One of the difficulties in tracing Don's journey is the multiple uses of the same name for different locations. Just as we have a Carroll, Iowa, Carroll, Illinois, and Carroll, Maryland, in Vietnam the name Tien Son might be used in different Districts and Provinces. This can be confusing to readers unfamiliar with Vietnamese political subdivisions. Also, names have changed through time. Names on 1970's vintage maps differ from those currently on Google Earth Pro or Google Maps. For important locations, I chose to provide both former and current place names if they were available.

A fourth issue concerned the use of language. During my stateside training, I was well accustomed to foul language both as a listener and speaker. However, "In-Country" verbiage brought the art to a much higher level. The f-bomb and creative modifications were commonly woven through many sentences. Likewise, racial slurs describing the enemy were the norm. I have deleted most of that language, not to deny the reality of the way it was, but to avoid unnecessarily offending potential readers. The exceptions are instances when using a substitution or euphemism would undermine the authenticity of what I am describing.

CHAPTER 2

I Have Myself Ready

During the early years of the war (1965 and 1966), about 20% of those killed in action were African Americans while the proportion of black Americans in the population was 11%. African American leaders complained to Lyndon Johnson about this injustice. In response, Johnson ordered the military to reduce the percentage of African Americans assigned to combat units. As a result, the black casualty rate was cut to 11.5% by 1969. When Don and I were drafted in 1968, this new policy was in full effect. I was not aware of this policy change and the effect it could have on me, a soon-to-be white college graduate inductee. I suspect Don Sparks was equally unaware.

MY TRANSITION TO THE ARMY

ALTHOUGH FRIENDS AND ACQUAINTANCES EXPLORED options for avoiding the draft, I never seriously considered voluntarily enlisting in the Air Force or Navy. I never considered crossing the border to Canada. Convinced by my brief ROTC experience at Iowa State that military life was not for me, I wanted to minimize whatever time I might need to serve. Therefore, I also ruled out joining the Army to gain the promise of a non-combat Military Occupational Specialty (MOS). If being drafted limited my service time to two years, then that was my preferred option. I didn't blame others for their choices and still don't. In hindsight, avoiding on-the-ground combat made good sense. I didn't really comprehend the risk I was taking and naively thought, "If I'm mandated to serve, I will. Then I'll get on with my life." Indeed, thanks in part to Dr. George Thomson, I had a life I was very much looking forward to.

Dr. Thomson was my academic advisor throughout my four-year enrollment in the Forestry Department at Iowa State University. As an advisor, friend, and life counselor, he had recommended me for a permanent job with the U.S. Forest Service, my first choice of employment. After graduation in May 1968, I started to work on the White Mountain National Forest in New Hampshire.

As a former Marine and WWII veteran, the District Ranger fully understood the impending consequences of my 1-A draft status. As a practical matter, he and my immediate supervisor decided not to invest time in the orientation and training normally given to new employees. Not surprisingly, a few months later, my mother called, and in a matter-of-fact conversation, said I had received my draft notice with orders to report on October 16, 1968.

I didn't bemoan this news. While I loved New Hampshire and the White Mountain National Forest, as a single man with no social life with people my own age, no girlfriend, and no prospects for either, I was ready to go. I really didn't appreciate what was coming, but whatever it was, I wanted to get it over with and go on with my life. Maybe I would go to graduate school after the Army.

Chapter 2

On a clear September morning, as the red maple leaves were just starting to change color, I left northern New Hampshire. Seeing New England foliage in its full fall splendor would have to wait till another year. I drove for 32 hours, straight to my parent's home near Prairie City, Iowa. Feeling very much alone and missing regular contact with many of my college friends, I tried to lighten my mood by listening to Mason Williams play *Classical Gas* on the radio. The fast-paced, upbeat tune sparked a sense of adventure—at least I tried to think of it that way.

I was sent to Ft. Polk, Louisiana for my Basic and Advanced Infantry Training at a place commonly referred to as Tigerland. Even though not even a tiger picture was in sight, the name was chosen, I suspect, to instill a mindset that graduates were headed for the jungle. As predicted by my ROTC experience, I hated military life. Again, it wasn't opposition to the Vietnam War; it was loss of the independence I had started to enjoy. While in the Army's control, I couldn't even take a walk. In my resentment, I didn't really grasp that the loss of freedom was preparation for life as an infantryman in a combat zone. There would be no solitary, get-away-from-it-all walks in the jungle.

When I received my Military Occupational Specialty at the end of Basic, I was shocked. I had assumed that I would be assigned to a job that would make use of my college education. But as I left the mess hall and unfolded the paper, I saw the 11B10 designation. I was going into the infantry. Quite likely, Johnson's racial adjustment policy had just landed on my naïve shoulders. I was participating in a more equal opportunity war. The period between receiving the 11 Bravo designation and my departure for Vietnam was one of the most pensive times in my young life. I could not help but wonder if I was saying a permanent good-bye to everyone and everything I had known.

While I was drafted first, I fell behind Donny in the race to the jungle by taking a brief sidetrack to non-commissioned officer (NCO) school in Ft. Benning, GA. Given my lack of self-confidence and assertiveness, I can't explain what made me think this would be a good idea. Spit-polishing boots that would be scuffed up the next day made no sense to me. Three weeks prior to graduation, a fellow NCO candidate from Iowa told me he was going to drop out. He didn't have to utter another word before I said, "Me too." We went to face the music together. Needless to say, our decision was not well received, and we received immediate reassignment to Vietnam as PFCs. In hindsight, had I finished the NCO training, I would have taken the responsibility very seriously. I would have done as well as many others. But at the time, I just didn't think so.

From June 10-20, 1969, I had ten days of leave to go home and say my good byes. I visited Dr. Thomson again; he had been a First Sergeant in the Army in World War II and a veteran of the Battle of the Bulge. I had visited him several times since being drafted, but this time was different since I was a few days away from leaving for Vietnam. If he was surprised or disappointed that I had dropped out of NCO school, he didn't show it. Instead, he gave me some advice about going to war that I appreciated so much, I still remember it. In essence, he said:

1. You won't do anyone any good dead. You have to do your duty, but you don't have to volunteer to put yourself at exceptional risk. In short, don't go out of your way trying to be a hero.

2. Try not to do anything you can't live with afterwards. (I now add to that, avoid failing to do what you know you should do. Although war suspends many of the laws and rules we commonly use to govern behavior, it should not override all rules of decent human conduct.)

3. Often the people who want to be in charge are not the best people for the job. I might be better off being the leader rather than being led by someone with poor character and skill.

As our visit ended, he offered to write to me, if I would write to him. I replied I would. Behind these promises was the sobering thought that my "escape and evasion" training was no guarantee of a safe return. I reassured myself that pilots, not infantrymen, were most vulnerable to capture.

My round of good-byes took me to Pleasant Hill Methodist Church where I tried to absorb every detail. I reflected on how I stood with God. Certainly I had not always lived the way I should have, but back in my youth I had been unwilling to commit to a more Godly way of life. I never really confessed my sins or asked for forgiveness. If I made it home, great. If I didn't, so be it. How naïve. I was not ready to meet my maker. Thankfully, God was merciful. I made it home and am now ready.

We had several family gatherings so I could see most of my relatives from both my mother's and father's families. I was very touched that my cousin Lee, his wife Zelda, and their baby daughter Rae Lyn came from Colorado. My Grandma Hart came to stay a few days before I left. Unfortunately, my sister and her family lived in Arizona so I didn't see them.

When it came to seeing old high school and college friends, the time was somewhat disappointing. I was beyond the stage of getting drunk and making a fool of myself with single friends. In fact, most of my high school friends were already married and settled into family life. My few friends at Iowa State were gone for the summer. On a previous leave I had been able to see Norm and Dorene Kammin and Craig and Becky Petre. Becky was an understanding friend who wrote to me several times during my tour in Vietnam—a kindness I still remember with gratitude.

At home I ran to stay in shape. I had been told that Vietnam was brutal, and I had to be in good shape to survive. I wanted to be ready. I wanted to make it home. Being prepared was almost an obsession. And, as I jogged the travel ways on the farm that had been my home since 1959, I tried to soak in all of comforting details.

On June 20, 1969, my parents and I rose early to go to the airport in Des Moines to begin my journey to Vietnam. Ironically, it was the very day Calvin and Arloha Sparks would be notified their son Don was missing in action. While it wasn't a great day for the Perkey family, it was the beginning of a very long nightmare for the Sparks family.

My grandmother took a picture of my mother Ruth, father Lynn, our dog Sheppy and me in the early morning hours before departing. I still treasure that fuzzy image of a moment in life that I will never forget. In a way, the picture captured a glimpse of similar scenes playing out across the country. When I touched Sheppy on the head as we were leaving, my Mom started to cry. I quickly moved on.

I don't remember much conversation during the trip to the airport; probably small talk to lessen the anxiety. Numb would be a fair description of my senses. My parents waited with me at the gate till it was time to say good-bye. I loved my mother and father, and they loved me. I had only seen my father cry on one other occasion; at my maternal grandfather's funeral. If I needed any confirmation that this was serious, that was it. My father never did tell me he loved me. Nor, did I ever tell him that I loved him. Nonetheless, love was there.

I recall sitting on that plane, listening to the engines rev up, feeling the plane's acceleration on the runway, followed by separation of the wheels from the ground. I was leaving my home and everything I had grown up with. At best, it was going to be a long, hard year. I wondered how I would do in combat, and if I would ever come home.

During my 10-day leave, I had connected with Barb, a girl I had dated a few times while a senior at Iowa State. Our relationship had never become serious, probably because she only wanted to be friends, and I was too shy and socially awkward to say I might have wanted more. Nevertheless, during my leave I wanted the feeling that someone other than my family cared about me. As it turned out, I would be departing from the Presidio near the Golden Gate Bridge, and Barb would be living nearby because she was starting a job in San Francisco. She invited me to spend my last night at her apartment, which I thought was great.

When I arrived at Barb's apartment about mid-afternoon, she wasn't there. Searching for a way to kill some time, I found a park that overlooked San Francisco Bay. It was a nice day and the scene was beautiful. I sat and reflected. After a few hours, I returned to Barb's apartment. She didn't seem that happy to see me. It was almost, "oh yes, I forgot you were coming." I exchanged pleasantries with several people in the apartment, but the conversation soon lagged. I was in uniform and with Berkeley located nearby where the war was extremely unpopular, soldiers received little respect. I felt unwelcome in the presence of Barb's friends.

I didn't eat that evening. I just sat alone on Barb's couch nursing a bottle of booze until I fell asleep. So much for my last night before shipping out.

I got up about 11 a.m. Saturday morning. When I knocked on Barb's door, she said "Come in."

"It's time for me to go."

"Do you want me to go with you to the bus stop?"

Chapter 2 29

"No."

"Well send me your address when you get there."

"Okay," I said, then kissed her on the cheek and left. It was hardly the heartfelt send-off I had hoped for. Feeling lonely, I caught a bus and was on my way to The Presidio, an Army base (now a National Park) that was a huge processing center for troops going to Vietnam. Although I didn't know it at the time, this was the same route taken by Don Sparks a little more than a month earlier.

Once on base, I tried again to talk my way out of my infantry assignment. At one issuing station, a man who never looked up, said in a sympathetic voice that with my 11 Bravo MOS there was no hope of my doing anything else. Perhaps his unusually kind response made me face reality. That was it. I needed to accept what was happening. And so, I became a reluctant warrior.

"What size boots do you wear?" I was asked at another distribution center.

"11N," I responded.

When a second pair of boots—11 R—was thrust into my hands, I protested, "I'm in the infantry. I need 11N."

"It doesn't matter, just go on," was the gruff reply.

When I was out of his sight, but still within range of long aisles of boot-filled shelves, I paused, not panicked, but determined. For a micro-second, I wondered if switching out the boots would be breaking the 8th commandment not to steal. Even more disconcerting was the specter of Ruth Perkey, former country-school teacher and strict disciplinarian. What would she think of her son taking such an uncharacteristic, assertive step? However, picturing my blistered, sore, aching feet trudging through the jungle evaporated my hesitation. I vaulted over the counter, quickly swapped those 11R boots for 11N, and rolled back over the counter.

I had always been the obedient, submissive son that Ruth and Lynn raised. But something was changing. As so many fellow soldiers had said about disobedient acts, "What are they going to do? Send you to Vietnam?" The last thing the Army wanted was any disciplinary action that would delay processing and flight out.

On July 3, 1969, I and others were taken by bus to the nearby airport at Oakland, CA. We boarded a commercial aircraft contracted to fly GIs to Vietnam. The after-dark stop for refueling in Alaska has been my only visit to our far-northern state, but stepping out of the plane and standing around in a Spartan shed while they filled-her up, hardly constituted a tourist moment.

On the morning of July 4th, I watched the aqua-colored water meet a sandy shore backed up with a brilliant green. It was beautiful. Following the shore at a safe distance brought us to our destination. When those wheels of the plane touched down and I felt the engines reverse thrust, it was my first GOOD MORNING VIETNAM moment, a phrase Robin Williams made famous years later in the movie of the same title.

DONNY'S TRANSITION TO THE ARMY

While I was in New Hampshire in the summer of 1968, Donny went on a twelve-country, Agricultural Tour in Europe to complete his course requirements for graduation. In an email communication, Ellis Macha, a fellow tour attendee from Iowa State, recalled:

> I really did not know Don, before we got to the YMCA in New York City. We flew in from Des Moines that day, landed at LaGuardia, and were bussed to the Y. None of my college friends were on the trip. So after we got our room assignments, I said to Don, "Are you ready to go?" He said, "Sure."
>
> We took off and used the subway to reach the Staten Island Ferry. We found the Empire State building and made it to the observation deck. I do not remember much after that, I suppose we went back to the Y and went to bed.
>
> The next morning our group followed the same path that Don and I had taken the night before with the addition of Wall Street and the Cathedral.

That evening we flew out of JFK to Portugal. Don and I spent all night drinking with the stewardess. We didn't even try to sleep.

> Ellis became a UH-1 helicopter pilot and went to Vietnam in March of 1970.

For the next two weeks or so, Don and I were inseparable, especially in the evenings. Somewhere around Belgium, we drifted apart. I am not sure why, I guess we just found others to party with.

After we returned to Ames and finished our written reports, I saw Don one more time, at one of the advisor's homes.

Little did Don know that interaction with people from other cultures on this European trip would be a forerunner to the communication challenges in his future.

Donny was drafted on December 3, 1968, before the lottery system was developed to make selection for the dubious induction honor more random. Don went to Fort Ord, California for his Basic Training. Like me, he was also tagged infantry, (MOS: 11B10). I suspect he was as shocked as I was. Had we seen each other, I'm sure we'd have used dry humor to console ourselves. If we thought freshman English at Iowa State was bad, how about this?

While in Basic Don broke his foot and missed part of the physical portion (marching) of his training. During my investigation, I learned his family had some anxiety about that. In my opinion, it wouldn't have been that critical, since basic was mostly about discipline and learning to be yelled at. I'm sure there were ample opportunities for that. Still, it's hard not to think, "What if?" What if he would have been recycled (repeated Basic); what if he had been delayed two months. Maybe he wouldn't have been in such a dangerous place at a dangerous time.

Jim Brinker remembers seeing Don when he was home on leave on New Year's Eve 1969. "Don was a great guy and a close friend of mine," Jim recounted to me. "We said goodbye on Highway 141 by Templeton, Iowa. New Year's Day morning was crisp and bright, just like our optimism for the future. He took the old 54 Chevy out for one last spin, said good bye to his family, and friends, and left."

Jim and Don corresponded. Don shared his thoughts before leaving for Vietnam, "Well this will be an adventure, and I have myself ready."

When I spoke with Jim's younger brother Clay, he told me the following story:

> I ate dinner with Don the evening before he left for Vietnam. It was at Toni's Restaurant on Highway 30 west of Carroll. We probably reminisced about all the good times at the Star-Line Ball Room. Don enjoyed the night life.

*Jim Brinker also went to Vietnam and became a decorated, WIA squad leader who later wrote a book titled **West of Hue.***

> We shook hands and wished each other well. He got in his Dad's pickup and drove down Highway 30. I never saw him again.
>
> Many years later, I encountered a Vietnam veteran at a gun show. He showed me a POW bracelet he was wearing. It had Don Sparks' name on it. I explained that Don and I were from the same home town and were best friends. He took the bracelet off and gave it to me. I still have it and treasure it.

Like me, Don had pre-Vietnam leave. Like me, he was not in a serious relationship with a girl. Our family and close friends were the relationships that mattered as we said our good-byes. Don't sister Esta, 16 at the time, recalls the trip to the Omaha airport as being quiet and somber. On the way home there was ominous silence. "Not a good feeling at all," she recalls. "Not a good feeling at all."

CHAPTER 3

CHERRY IN THE BUSH

MY ENTRY INTO VIETNAM

I arrived in Vietnam on July 4, 1969, not that the holiday mattered in a war zone. The only fireworks that day was a rocket exploding inside the compound at Bien Hoa[3]. Fortunately, there was no injury or damage. I was surprised, however, that the enemy could get close enough to fire a rocket into such a developed and relatively secure area.

During the next two and a half weeks, I completed my in-country processing. Most of the time was spent shuffling from place to place with little knowledge of what was coming next.

I had been carefully hanging onto the "pilfered" pair of 11N boots I had obtained at the expense of my mother's reputation as a child raiser. Surprise, surprise! I was told to hand them over. To assure a supply of replacement boots, each arriving soldier was instructed to carry an extra pair, which was promptly added to a general stockpile. My effort to prepare proved futile, but I have remembered that "growth" experience as a life lesson. Worrying is seldom effective, since things seldom go as anticipated.

---

3 Bien Hoa was the Division Headquarters for the 1st Air Cavalry.

In the absence of specific official information, rumors circulated that most grunts (anyone with an 11 Bravo MOS like me) were being assigned to either the 1st Air Cavalry or the 101st Airborne. The rumor was validated when I was assigned to the 1st Air Cavalry, operating north of Saigon along the Cambodian border.

On July 20, shortly before Neil Armstrong, Buzz Aldren, and Mike Collins landed on the moon, I and three other new grunts were at the 1st Battalion, 8th Cav. Base at Quan Loi, receiving our last words of encouragement before departing on a Huey to join our company in the bush. A Major emphasized how fortunate we were to have been assigned to the 1st Air Cav. The Cav had more helicopters than any other outfit, so if wounded, we had the best chance of quickly receiving good medical attention. I accepted that as fact, and maybe it was a better send off than just saying "good luck," but truthfully, it wasn't that reassuring. My expression probably conveyed, "Oh, OK, that's great. My mother will be glad to read that in my next letter home."

I suspect the intention of his farewell speech was to reduce the occurrence of guys getting cold feet when it came time to leave for the bush. Earlier in the processing period I had encountered a soldier I recognized from my Advanced Infantry Company at Ft. Polk. When I asked what he was doing, he explained, "I'm still here at battalion. I refused to get on the helicopter for the cherry ride." I was shocked. Switching a pair of boots suddenly fell to the bottom of the "disobedient scale." I don't know what if anything was done to him. Clearly, he hadn't been motivated by those lame assurances, "now come on son, it won't be that bad" and "you don't want to let the folks back home down do you?"

I was trained as light weapons infantry and assigned to an air mobile unit. On-the-job training was the norm. Watch what others do and try to do the same.

When I entered a Huey for my maiden voyage to the boonies, it was my first time in a helicopter. Hueys flew with no doors and to fully utilize the load capacity of the air craft two occupants sat on the floor with feet hanging out into the wild blue yonder. What a contrast to life in the state-side Army, where such risky behavior would never be tolerated. The underlying message was clear. In a combat zone, grunts were expendable. If one perished, the specifics of how it happened would probably never have to be explained.

Chapter 3

As we descended toward the jungle canopy, I first spotted yellow smoke and then men below. The Huey hovered above the ground as we jumped out. A few supplies were quickly kicked out, and the helicopter lifted off. One of the men who approached was slightly older, and his jungle fatigues were fresher and cleaner in contrast to the faded fatigues and helmet covers of others in the welcoming party. The best dressed said, "I am Captain Pate, your company commander. You will each go with your assigned squad leader. Listen to these men. They are going to teach you how to live out here." He was much more aloof than the encouraging happy Major back at the Cav base. Captain Pate wasn't as bad as officers encountered in the States during training. However, I knew he wasn't approachable. Still I got his message loud and clear. If we didn't pay close attention we were more likely to go home in a body bag.

In contrast to Captain Pate's aloofness was Squad Leader Jim Hughes' warmness. Jim brought me into the company perimeter and introduced me to the other squad members. I was swamped with questions like, "where are you from in The World? What kind of cigarettes do you smoke? What kind of bravos & sierras (beer and soda) do you like?" The last two questions relate to who in the squad you will compete with on log day. Besides Jim, there was "Groovy" Jerry R. Reeves, Borax, Squirrel, Tyack, Pineapple, Lucky, and Little Joe. We were in the 4th Platoon, the weapons platoon, meaning we had an 81 mm mortar and a recoilless rifle to hump around instead of a machine gun. I thought, "Wait a minute. My MOS is 11B, not 11C. I don't know how to do mortars." "Well, never mind, you will learn."

The landscape we operated in had modest changes of elevation. Vegetation was mostly jungle interspersed with small, wet, grass-covered openings. Intermingled were abandoned rubber plantations. Most of the population was clustered in villages and cities. Outside those populated areas, any Vietnamese encountered was considered unfriendly. Unless told differently, we were in what was referred to as a free fire zone.

The first night I hooched with two other guys, a temporary arrangement before I was paired with Little Joe. My new hooch-mate taught me the art and science of putting two ponchos together with some freshly cut bamboo stakes to make a decent place to sleep at night.

Little Joe was short not only in stature, but also in time left to serve in Vietnam. He had hoped to spend the remainder of his time in a job at the rear. When they sent him back to the boonies instead, he became absolutely paranoid; convinced before his remaining time was over, he would be seriously wounded or killed.

I was a very sound sleeper. The third morning in the bush, I was awakened by an explosion. I looked up, and Little Joe wasn't there. I grabbed my M-16 and darted out of the hooch. We were being mortared. Everyone else was already in foxholes. They'd heard that distant telltale pop. There was no room in the trenches for me. Squad leader Jim Hughes saw the bewildered look on my face and told me, "Lie just as flat to that ground as you can." The exploding rounds came closer and closer. I could hear the shrapnel flying through the bamboo. "The next one was going to be right on us," I thought. "So, this is what it's like." Thank God, the shelling stopped.

After that morning, I noticed that Little Joe had moved from the hooch to the foxhole, fearing he might not make it to cover if we were mortared again. "My God," I thought. "I may die out here, but I won't live like that for a year." In a couple weeks, Little Joe left, and as far as I know, stayed in the rear until he got on the Freedom Bird and went back to The World. Little Joe was not the only one to suffer from that "nearing the end of tour" paranoia, but he had the most severe case I witnessed.

With my relatively clean helmet, I stuck out like a sore thumb. Basically, I was still a Cherry, untested in a real fire fight; with a lot to learn about surviving in a combat zone. Shortly before I arrived in the boonies, a guy named Green had been shot in the leg while he was outside the perimeter doing his morning bathroom business. Consequently, every morning when I took my turn going out with the entrenching tool, I had someone reminding me not to go too far. This was part of what Captain Pate meant by "learn how to live out here."

One day, we were humping along when we heard firing a moderate distance away. We stopped and lay prone for a short time before backing up and spreading out with a considerable (out-of-sight) distance between us. Another platoon in our company was in contact with the enemy, and soon I heard the sound of movement in the jungle. The firing had stopped. The sound of people thrashing through the jungle was coming closer and moving at a good rate. I surmised it was the enemy breaking contact and running before artillery fire or gunships could arrive. I couldn't see them through the dense jungle. However, I knew they were close enough that if I fired they would return fire. The only person near me was a city kid from Boston; even newer to the bush than I was. He wasn't adapting well to life in the boonies, and I wasn't sure he'd help me if the enemy fired on us, so I didn't shoot.

That evening, as I reflected on what had happened, I decided I should have fired. The rest of the squad would have come to help me. I had new guy qualms, and therefore, had not done what I was supposed to. I saw Jim Hughes, my squad leader sitting alone and decided to tell him what happened.

"Have you told anyone else about this?"

"No."

"Then don't. Keep your mouth absolutely shut. And the next time, just do it."

We never spoke of it again. Initially, I thought he was worried about the company commander finding out and being mad. Later, I realized he was probably as worried about what others in the squad might think about my reluctance to fire. As a cherry, I was still earning the respect of the squad. Jim didn't want the incident to undermine others' confidence in me. He was still helping me integrate into the group, and no purpose would be served by waving a red flag about my reliability under fire.

On log (resupply) day, Jim told us the armorer was coming to the field. If any of us had issues with our weapons, now was the time to have them checked. My M16 didn't seem to be functioning quite right, so Jim took it to the armorer. Later, when I asked about it, Jim said, "You were correct. They took it back to the rear to be worked on."

A decision had been made to phase out the heavy weapons (mortar and recoilless rifle). Jim pointed to an M60 machine gun that was replacing the mortar and asked, "Do you want to carry that?" He then explained the benefits of being a machine gunner. First and foremost, I wouldn't have to walk point. Also, I wouldn't have to carry trip flares and claymores, so while everyone else was setting up the night defensive position, I could relax and clean the machine gun. At first, I said, "No," thinking I would stick with my M-16.

"You want a weapon, don't you?" Jim asked.

With a puzzled look, I hesitantly replied, "Yes."

Pointing at the machine gun, he bluntly stated, "Well, there it is."

In Jim's diplomatic way, he went on to sweeten the pot by telling me that if I carried it for two months, he would then move it to someone else. I had just experienced a sudden, unexpected career change. I later learned that because of my size, he figured I could manage to carry it better than most guys in the squad. Apparently, he had lost any concerns about my earlier hesitation to fire at the enemy.

Over time, Jim and I became friends. We liked many of the same things so we became good trading/bargaining partners. We both smoked Salem cigarettes and with only so many packs available, we had to share. My mother sent me red licorice in care packages, which Jim also loved. So I shared that. Our mutual love of chocolate milk was irrelevant until we had the opportunity to provide security at the Landing Zone where luxuries like cold milk were available. Then, Jim used his influence to obtain a quart for him and one for me. The fact that he was a sergeant and I was a PFC didn't matter. We were in this together and we shared.

DON'S ENTRY INTO VIETNAM

Don's tour in Vietnam started on May 13, 1969. As Don started his in-country processing, he wouldn't have known the company he was destined to serve with had been involved in a fierce engagement called "The Battle for Nui Yon Hill." According to Executive Officer Jim Gordon, "On May 13, 14 and 15, Company C was reduced from about 80 people in the bush to about 30. They had 12 KIA and 30 WIA. May 13, SP-4 Larry Aiken, 2nd Platoon was listed as MIA. In short, the 1st and 2nd Platoons of C Company had been decimated. Many of the company's experienced soldiers were either dead or wounded. The completion of Don's in-country processing and training aligned perfectly with the need to fill vacancies created by that battle.

On May 30, 1969, Don, along with five other soldiers, was assigned to C Company, 3rd BN. It is not known when these six newcomers joined the company in the field, but Marvin Timperley remembers they were taken from Chu Lai to somewhere in the bush in Quang Tin Province[4], in the northern portion of what was South Vietnam. Rice was the primary crop in the broad valleys. The steeper foothills were jungle covered. It was a very dangerous area.

---

4   Now Quang Nam Province.

Dogs sense things, and Sheppy wanted to be part of my departure on June 20, 1969.

My squad members, October 1969
FRONT: *Squad Leader Jim Hughes;* 2ND ROW, *l-r: Jerry Reeves, Oscar Gaines, Arlyn Perkey;* 3RD ROW, L-R: *Jeff Croston, Bob Strenz, Pat Toon, Bryan Tyack, Gary Borkowski;* BACK: *Marcel Gorre Chuck Deaton was killed about 3 weeks before this picture was taken.*

Chapter 3

The Helicopter was used extensively for many purposes, including insertion and extraction of troops from the jungle. Gary Borkowski (kneeling center right), is carrying full pack and gear. The soldier in the foreground holds his helmet to avoid losing it in the wind created by the revolving helicopter blades. He will have to wait to replace his torn fatigues until clean clothes are brought out for everyone.

By necessity, the dress code in the bush was relaxed. This picture in a rubber plantation shows how we looked after humping those packs. L-R: *Arlyn Perkey, Jerry Reeves, Gary Borkowski, and Bryan Tyack.*
PHOTOGRAPH COURTESY OF GARY BORKOWSKI

Den, a Kit Carson scout assigned to our company, is standing in a relatively mature growth of bamboo. Many Kit Carson scouts were former NVA who had decided to Choi Hoi, that is to defect to South Vietnam. I have always wondered if Den survived re-education after the Fall of Saigon.
PHOTOGRAPH COURTESY OF WEBEWEBBIERS

Chapter 3

Third Platoon Leader, Staff Sergeant David Stanley (foreground) and Sergeant Tom Coker receive our mail (red bags) at LZ Ellen. To a grunt, mail from The World was an even bigger morale booster than bravos and sierras (beer and soda).

This shows the density of the jungle we cut our way through and illustrates why we couldn't see muzzle flashes from shots fired from bunkers 25 yards away. Notice the pack on the ground left of center. Now look for the face of the grunt along the left edge (center). He is writing a letter to someone in The World.

PHOTOGRAPH COURTESY OF WEBEWEBBIERS

RTO on Ground: Smoke is out
Pilot: Smoke is yellow
RTO on Ground: Roger that
Grunt lower left holds up M16 for Huey pilots to sight on for landing;
Cobra gunship in distant background provides security.
Maybe there will be mail and bravos and sierras.

L-R: Oscar Gaines "Squirrel," Moun, a "Kit Carson Scout"
and Marcel "Pineapple" Gorre. When I was wounded,
Pineapple helped me with my bandage while under fire.
Later, when Squirrel walked by, we exchanged facial expressions,
no words. The leaves in the background are bamboo.
PHOTOGRAPH COURTESY OF WEBEWEBBIERS

Chapter 3

Don Ketcham is standing on the left with his hands crossed. Captain Cary Perkins (center, 1st Cav. patch on upper left arm) spoke to me once, after I was wounded. I will never forget his words: "It is all over for you. You are going home. Say your good-byes. You won't be coming back out here."

PHOTOGRAPH COURTESY OF WEBEWEBBIERS

Captain Perkins was correct, 2 weeks later, I was one very blessed grunt; home with my million-dollar wound. I was looking at the slides I had taken in Vietnam, then reading, then napping. The aluminum gismo on my arm was to prevent atrophy. Don Sparks never had this moment.

*Three young grunts, October 1969, in the rear
(Quan Loi) for a brief in-country R & R. L-R: Jerry Reeves,
Gary Borkowski, Arlyn Perkey — We smiled then.*

*Forty-eight years later, the same 3 old grunts re-convened
and shared memories. We gave up the beads and cigarettes.
Oh yes, we changed the color of our hair. L-R: Arlyn Perkey,
Gary Borkowski, Jerry Reeves — We are all still smiling.*

CHAPTER 4

AN EYE FOR AN EYE

> For grunts in the jungle, the motivation behind various fire fights was unclear. Often it seemed to be little more than retaliation. Whenever we inflicted a loss on them, they tried hard to inflict a loss on us. We ambushed them; they ambushed us. No perceptible strategic or tactical advantage was gained or lost with each event. However, the wounded were no less wounded; the dead no less dead.

NINETEEN-YEAR-OLD CHUCK DEATON from Klamath Falls, Oregon, arrived in Vietnam on July 27, 1969, and was assigned to Delta Company in late August. Chuck joined my squad and was paired to hooch with Marcel "Pineapple" Gorre[5]. Chuck was new to the jungle, and Pineapple became Chuck's mentor on surviving in the bush.

Our squad was divided into two fire teams. Initially Pineapple walked point for one and Bryan Tyack for the other. In late September, Chuck replaced Pineapple as point man for his fire team. At that time, we were working out of LZ Jerri, near the village of Bu Dop on the Cambodian border. On September 27, we found an area with very active trail usage on the north side of the Song Be.

After establishing a perimeter and stopping for lunch, Delta Company commander Captain Folsom sent my fire team with Tyack on point to patrol the perimeter. Our four-man team included the soldier carrying the radio for 4th Platoon, me with the M60 machine gun, and my assistant gunner, Gary Borkowski, walking drag. As we crossed heavily used trails, I thought, "Wow, this area is really dangerous." We had walked for a distance when Tyack suddenly stopped, turned around, and announced, "I lost the compass. I don't know where we are." I was dumbfounded. As a forester experienced in navigating through woods, I probably knew better than the rest how serious—and dangerous—the situation was.

The dense jungle canopy obscured the cloudy sky, giving us no clues to regain our bearings and find our way back toward the defensive perimeter. Simply following a trail and hoping for the best was definitely a bad idea. Thank God, we had the radio. Reluctantly we reported our dilemma and were told to stand by and await further instructions. After an interminable wait, they finally said, "Fire a shot in the air so we have an idea what direction and how far away you are." We fired letting them know our general location, but we still had no idea about which direction would bring us closer to safety. We tried again. We wandered. We repeated this process four or five times, but accomplished nothing. The longer this went on and knowing how vulnerable we were, the more worried (frightened) I became. Even so, I imagined what the NVA

---

5   During my 2017 conversation with Marcel Gorre, I said, "It's hard for me to call you anything but 'Pineapple' even though I know now how insensitive that is." We chuckled about today's insistence on political correctness in the "The World" and went on with our conversation. Marcel's appearance suggests he has Asian-Pacific Islander origins; hence his nickname. In Vietnam, most of us had nicknames, some of which would be considered awful today. In most cases, no disrespect was intended, and that was certainly true of Pineapple who was greatly admired.

must be wondering as they listened to these periodic single shots in slightly different locations. Had their enemy lost their minds? Or, was one of their comrades wandering around doing something stupid?

Eventually, Captain Folsom had no choice but to reveal his location. After they fired three or four shots, we were able to find our way back to safety. Our squad leader Jim Hughes was kind, but let us know Captain Folsom was furious, because he had to give away his position. We packed up, moved to a new night location, and set up an ambush with Claymore mines on a trail.

As dusk neared, I was startled by an explosion that sent me scrambling to the M60. Someone in the adjoining 1st Platoon had detonated one of the Claymores we had set. Aiming down the trail, I followed with a burst from the M60. After a few minutes there was a radio call wanting to know if I had actually seen a target. I said, "No. I just fired in the general direction." That was fine. We in 4th Platoon didn't know at the time that one of two enemy in the area had escaped.

Darkness came and Gary Borkowski and I were in our hooch. In the stillness, we could hear groaning. The ambush had worked, but someone was still alive. It became pitch black and the groaning continued. Finally, it stopped. Death eventually, mercifully had arrived. Almost 20 years later at a reunion, Jim Hughes and I recalled the incident. I said, "I wish one of us could have put him out of his misery." Of course, that would have been neither allowable nor feasible, but my ingrained Iowa-farm ethic didn't let animals suffer. How less acceptable was this human suffering?

When I was in basic training, we often marched to the cadence of "Poison Ivy," a tune by The Coasters. Not only was the rhythm suitable, but the words substituted for the lyrics imprinted the significance of what we would be facing. As happened on the night of September 27, "late at night while you're sleepin', Charlie Cong comes creepin' aro-
-und."

The next morning, we found the body of a Viet Cong carrying an M16 with the old-style open flash suppressor. Captain Folsom decided to send out a small reconnaissance, but told Jim Hughes not to send the idiots who got lost. This time Pineapple's fire team was sent with Chuck Deaton walking point. They were to stay fairly close to our established defensive perimeter, a worrisome situation in which everyone inside the perimeter must be aware that "friendlies" would be passing nearby. While the fire team was on patrol, Jerry Reeves was sent out to retrieve supplies that had just arrived on a "log bird."

Sometime during the night or very early morning hours, the VC who had escaped the previous day's ambush had led others back to our perimeter and set up very tight to it. Pineapple's team walked into them and was ambushed with a Claymore mine and gunfire. Chuck was gunshot in the chest; Bob had shrapnel in his hand. Pineapple thought the firing was friendly fire from our own defensive perimeter. He screamed for the firing to stop. Pineapple made his way to Chuck and tried everything he could—including mouth-to-mouth resuscitation—to deal with the sucking chest wound. But none of his efforts could save his friend's life. Chuck was unable to speak before he passed. It is hard for me to imagine how the enemy managed to get that Claymore mine into position to execute that ambush so close to our perimeter without being detected. They were quiet and courageous.

Jerry, who was still outside the perimeter, low crawled back, screaming, "Don't shoot. Don't shoot."

I saw Pineapple after Bob Strenz was Medevacked along with Chuck's body. He was devastated. When I spoke with Pineapple 48 years later, he said, "I was a changed person after September 28, 1969. I lost my innocence that day. Last year, I went back to Klamath Memorial Park, the cemetery where Chuck is buried," Pineapple continued. "I'm glad I did. I had a chance to say a final good-bye. I felt better after that."

I didn't know Chuck well. I hadn't had much direct contact with him during the brief time he had been in our squad. However, his death brought home the reality of the danger I was facing. I had been in the field about two months; this was the first and only person killed from my squad while I was there. The possibility of my own death on any day was unavoidably in front of me. I had never been predisposed to express my thoughts on paper. However, a few days after this incident, I wrote the following and carried it in my water-tight ammo box until I was wounded. It was later returned to me with my few other personal belongings.

DEATON'S DEATH

Dusk settles down on the new night loc
Ponchos are spread in night's preparation
Jokes float around in the still evening air
Life is alive in our home of desolation.

Pop! Aww! Boom! Boom!
"Quiet, listen, for sound indications."
A wheezing moan to the rhythm of breath.
It stopped; Victory to the Americans, a gook is dead.

Morning sun in an old night loc
Cocoa's the way to start a new day
Patrol's going out to get information
Routine's not romance to a grunt's way of thinkin'

Watching and waiting, dreaming and thinking
Moments meander, no alarm, no sensation.
Boom! Boom! Crack! Crack! Crack!
What's that? What happened? Who's where? Who's what?

Medevac! Medevac! Thirty-three hundred.
The tables are turning, but questions remaining,
Which ones? Which ones? Will go from our midst.
Bob is just wounded, but Deaton is dead.[6]

---

6 I've been asked why Deaton's death affected me so much, even though I knew of other fatalities. The only people most infantrymen knew well were other squad members, because a squad had to stay together all the time. We couldn't just go talk to someone else in another squad even in the same platoon, let alone another platoon. For example, on December 9, one of the wounded was in the squad immediately behind us. When I recently saw his picture on a web site, he looked familiar. However, I certainly didn't know him, and if his name wasn't listed as WIA that day, I wouldn't know anything about his being there. Similarly, I didn't know the three men killed in the events described in "Bait." I watched their bodies go out in a body bag and that was sobering. In contrast, Chuck Deaton was in my squad, so his death was much more personal. Chuck was the only person in my squad killed while I was in Vietnam. I don't mean to sound callus about the others, but it didn't have the same effect on me.

CHAPTER 5

BAIT

IN 1969, INFANTRYMEN WERE LARGELY ENGAGED in guerilla warfare. U.S. forces had far superior fire power than the NVA and VC. Artillery fire, fixed-wing aircraft, and helicopter gunships were routinely dispatched to enemy locations—when they could be found. The enemy had the advantage of elusiveness. Often, they could be found only when they chose to initiate contact, typically when they could inflict casualties and quickly withdraw before superior U.S. firepower could arrive. Infantry units were essentially used as bait to lure enemy troops to reveal their location.

Many fire fights were brief skirmishes, dangerous for the people directly involved on both sides, but of little consequence in terms of any long-standing control of territory or population. As described in "An Eye for An Eye," the Viet Cong ambushed us; we ambushed them. More often than not, however, they had the advantage of firing first and inflicting the first casualties. Although the specifics of each encounter with the enemy were unique, all had dire consequences for those involved. Few, however, resulted in a U.S. infantryman being taken as a POW as Don had been on June 17.

In this chapter, I recount the sequence of events leading to an ambush of my squad on December 9 and the consequences I experienced. My intent is to convey the nature of guerilla warfare and how quickly a small-incident of infantry engagement could turn deadly. As I write about these incidents, it is hard to believe that almost 50 years have passed. Naturally, many details have faded, but in an attempt to be as accurate as possible, I consulted WeBeWebbiers, an internet site maintained by Gordon Swenson, a veteran of Delta Company. In addition, I had an opportunity to meet and reminisce with fellow squad members Gary Borkowski and Jerry Reeves in September 2017. Some of our memories matched; others revealed details I had not known or misremembered. What follows, then, is to the best of my ability, a faithful reconstruction of events.

As indicated by the charts in Appendix 2a and 2b, casualties and personnel turnover resulted in on-going realignment of platoons and squads. By late November, Delta Company's 4th Platoon had evolved into the 3-2 squad of the 3rd Platoon. Jim Hughes had departed for *"The World,"* and Marcel "Pineapple" Gorre had become the leader of my squad.

****

December 1. Delta Company combat assaulted from LZ Ellen into a mixed jungle and swamp area south and east of the meandering Song Be. *(Map 1)*

December 2. The 3rd Platoon separated from the rest of the company and traversed an especially nasty swamp where we encountered not only traditional land leeches, but fat slimy water leeches that I knocked off before they could attach to my legs. We revisited the site of a two-month old skirmish. Although we never buried enemy dead, the enemy must have returned and attended to the unpleasant duty.

December 4. We re-joined the Command Post and 1st Platoon.

December 5. We moved out with our heavies in the morning. At 8:20 a.m., 1st Platoon, on point, spotted the enemy and fired; a relatively unusual contact initiated by us. Enemy return fire from a machine gun and an AK-47 hit Thomas Bowman in both legs. The command and control helicopter was in the area and Medevacked Bowman. Artillery was called in on the enemy bunkers in the area.

Chapter 5

MAP 1
AMBUSH SITES ALONG THE SONG BE

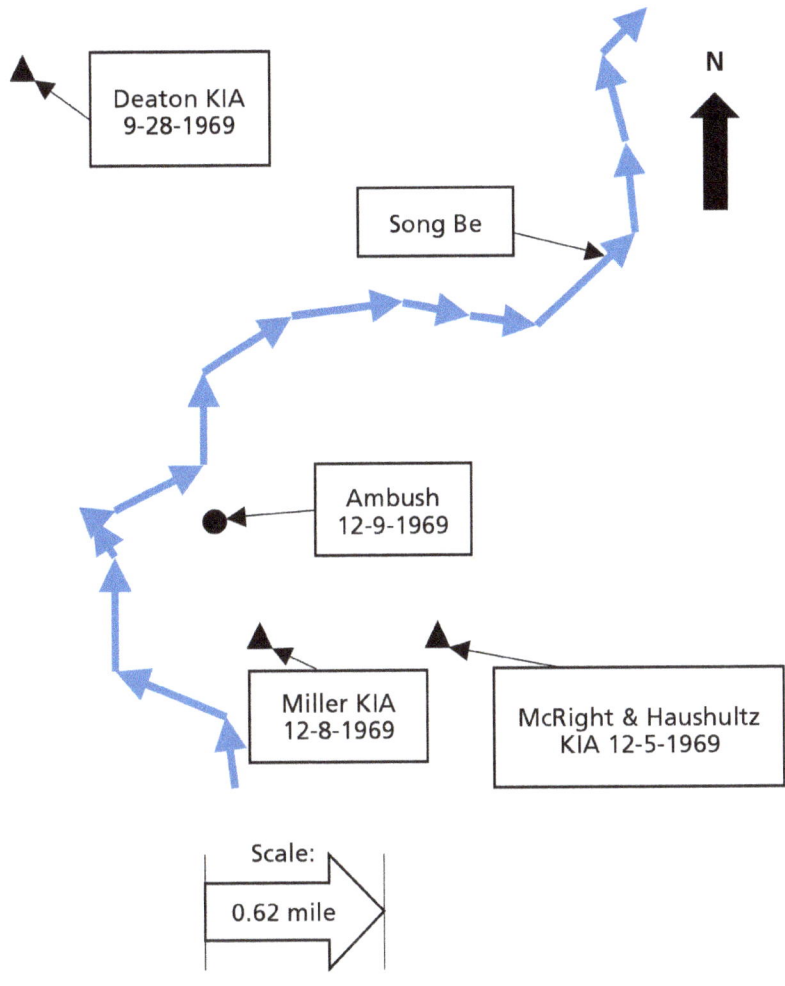

About 11 a.m. 1st Platoon was attacked and suffered casualties, before they could call for an air strike.

We in 3rd Platoon had been moving forward in single file when the firing started. We hit the ground, dropped our heavies, and waited.

I heard occasional rounds cracking through the air, but wasn't sure if it was sniper fire purposely directed at us or stray shots from 1st Platoon's contact.

After a few minutes, we moved forward again, "light" (weapons, ammo, & some water). Carrying the machine gun on my shoulder, I followed squad-mate Danny Smith. The forward pace was slow, moving a few steps while staying low and then stopping. By now, I was convinced we were being shot at, but had no idea where the source was. We approached a larger than average opening in the jungle where we paused as one person at a time would run across. When Danny's time to cross came, he hesitated. I knew he was waiting too long and we were likely to lose sight of the person ahead which would not be good. Finally, I said, "Danny, we have to go." He took off and went as fast as he could. I thought, "God I hope he makes it," and was relieved when he did. Now it was my turn, and I didn't like the idea any more than Danny had, especially since it is hard to run and stay low while carrying a machine gun.

Recalling that incident after so many years, I am somewhat surprised. I had dropped out of NCO School, because I lacked the confidence and desire to tell others what to do in combat. Yet, in the moment of Danny's hesitation, I found within myself what I now call "reluctant, modestly assertive, not-much-choice leadership."

Our Platoon advanced to where we aligned adjacent to the 1st Platoon's position. I set up the machine gun facing the contact and lay prone behind it. There was no overhead cover. Suddenly I heard a loud noise behind me and rolled on my side to see an F-100 jet coming down. Generally, we did not have fixed-wing air support. But that day, our forward observer's request had been approved. Although I didn't see it, the

> **1ST PLATOON CASUALTIES**
>
> Roger McRight, Tinley Park, IL was shot and killed.
>
> Peter Dripps received a head wound when a round struck his helmet.
>
> Medic Jerry Hauschultz, Marion, WI, tried to crawl forward to reach McRight. He was shot and killed.
>
> Kelly Dupree had a broken collarbone.
>
> Lonnie "Lucky" Hartline had a finger shot off.

Chapter 5   *57*

F100 was probably accompanied by Snoopy, a spotter plane that fired a white phosphorous round to identify the target's location. The jet came close enough that I could glimpse the pilot's face, and he seemed to be looking right at me. I hoped he knew what he was doing as he repeatedly swooped down, dropped a bomb, and pulled up and away.

We finally closed in with 1st Platoon and received the bad news that two men had been killed. We were to help provide security for the evacuation of the 1st Platoon wounded. Among the wounded was Lonnie "Lucky" Hartline a former platoon-mate. Seated in a sling, he was being winched up through the canopy to a Medevac helicopter. [7]

With the wounded evacuated, 1st Platoon carried the body bags with Roger McRight and Jerry Haushultz until the evening when we came to an opening around old bomb craters. Because Medevac helicopters had sophisticated hoisting equipment, they were reserved for airlifting casualties. In contrast, the helicopter that would be transporting Roger and Jerry on their last ride lacked such sophisticated equipment. Unable to land in such a confined space, the helicopter lowered two cables that were attached to the body bags lying on the edge of a water-filled bomb crater. As the helicopter lifted off, the bags were dragged into the water for an irreverent dunking. An alert officer immediately jumped into the water and tried to cradle the bags until the helicopter gained elevation and broke through the upper jungle canopy.

I know the helicopter crew intended no disrespect, but to grunts who could encounter the same fate, it was no morale booster. Even in death, the jungle yielded little respect; tribute could wait. Getting them out before dark took precedence over respect for the dead. I didn't know either of the men personally, but I thought about their families who did not yet know their loved ones had just been killed in action.

---

7   In August, Lucky and I had been together in 4th Platoon. We had been inserted at the outskirts of the city of An Loc. While waiting for instructions, my squad was standing in a circle talking. For whatever reason, Lucky pulled out a knife, and without intending any harm, aimed it at the ground between my feet. Unfortunately his aim was off and it stuck into my left foot. I didn't know how badly I was injured until later when we set up our night location and I removed my boot. The knife had gone between two toes, gashing each. The medic sewed up the gashes, and fortunately the wound never became infected. The Army doesn't award a purple heart for "friendly" knife throwing in combat. I didn't even get any time off in the rear. However, I do have two small scars and a lighter than average combat story to tell. In this December 5 incident, Lucky returned to the Command Post to have his hand bandaged. When asked what happened, Lucky said, "That SOB shot my finger off." With that, he grabbed his weapon and went back into the fight.

December 6. A helicopter gunship fired on the December 5 contact area and received return fire. An additional airstrike was called in while we waited about 500 meters away. Our subsequent search of bunkers on site confirmed although they were old, they had recently been used.

December 7. 1st Platoon was re-supplied and our Company Commander, Spencer Folsom was evacuated with a relapse of malaria. He was replaced by Captain Cary Perkins. We humped northwest about 1500 meters and established a night location 400 meters east of the Song Be. My 3rd Platoon established a separate night location about 300 meters farther east of the river.

December 8. In the morning, 1st Platoon moved out with Randy Miller walking point. At 9:07 a.m., Randy circled a bomb crater, walked 15 feet into the bush, and was shot in the leg. He made it back to the perimeter established by the rest of the platoon. At 9:10 a.m., contact was broken and a Medevac was urgently requested for Randy who had gone into shock. When Randy was hoisted into the helicopter, one of the crew looked back and shook his head. Artillery and air strikes were called to support those remaining in the field.

> Randall D. Miller from Danville, West Virginia was pronounced dead on arrival when the helicopter landed at Quan Loi.

In the afternoon, we crossed a stream and walked into the most extensive, active bunker complex I had seen since arriving in Vietnam. The enemy's withdrawal had been hasty, and they had left behind cooking utensils as well as an AK-47 and an SKS rifle.

We set up our night location within the complex; our section of the defensive perimeter was fairly close to the stream. After our evening meal, we were told we would be the point squad in the morning. I knew the next day was going to be bad. The loss of this important site would make life harder for the North Vietnamese soldiers, motivating a retaliatory strike. Walking point would be especially dangerous, and I thought, "Why us? Who says it is our turn?" Considering the three KIA from 1st Platoon in the last few days, this wasn't a fair thought, and I laid it aside.

I tried not to think the worst, but I wrote a letter to my parents, assuming that if I didn't survive, the letter would be found in my weathertight ammo box and forwarded to them. In a recent conversation with my hooch mate Gary Borkowski, I learned that he also wrote a letter home that night. We may have talked about the ominous outlook for the next day. As if I needed additional reason to be concerned, just before dark a trip flare we had set at the outskirts of our perimeter went off. Nobody on guard duty responded by blowing a Claymore, but there was little doubt the enemy had probed our position and pinpointed our exact location. They would be waiting to ambush us the next morning.

Before falling asleep, I mentally rehearsed exactly what I would do when the first shots rang out: collapse to my knees; roll the gun off my shoulder; slip my arms from my pack; remove a 100-round belt of ammunition I carried across the top; set up the gun; lie prone behind it; begin firing. Reminding myself that further worry wouldn't help and being exhausted at the end of a long day of humping, I fell into a reasonably deep sleep.

December 9. The morning began as usual with a cup of instant hot chocolate and a can of C-ration fruit. Nervously, I again rehearsed the steps I would follow when the firing began. When word came to "saddle up," I was as ready as I could be. Our squad was given a zig-zagging compass course to follow, presumably making it more difficult for the enemy to get a good read on exactly where we were going.

We moved out, following newly appointed point man, Pat Toon. He was backed up by relatively fresh instant NCO SGT Don "Ketch" Ketcham, with relatively new Danny Smith next in line with an M-79 grenade launcher. Experienced Squad Leader Marcel "Pineapple" Gorre was in front of me and Assistant Gunner Gary Borkowski was behind. Bryan Tyack, and Jerry Reeves were on drag. The 3-3 squad was next in line. About 250 meters out, as Pat, Ketch, and Danny made the first zig in our compass course, the firing began. Miraculously, Pat

> **SQUAD MEMBERS INVOLVED IN DECEMBER 9 INCIDENT**
>
> Marcel "Pineapple" Gorre, Squad Leader
>
> **SQUAD MEMBERS**
>
> Arlyn Perkey
> Gary Borkowski
> Don "Ketch" Ketcham
> Jerry Reeves
> Danny Smith
> Pat Toon
> Bryan Tyack

MAP 2
LOCATION OF DECEMBER 9, 1969 AMBUSH
Arlyn Perkey Wounded in Action

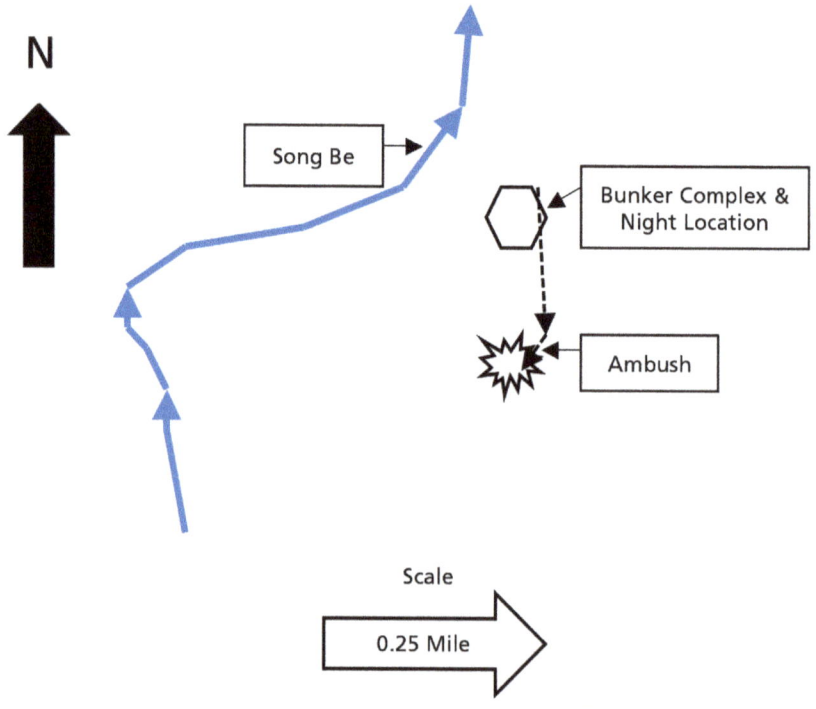

was not hit in the initial burst that sent a round through a large tree root, then into Ketch's left leg.

As I followed the plan I had mentally rehearsed, I heard a voice saying someone had been shot. I passed down the line that we had one man down. Jerry Reeves remembers hearing Platoon Leader David Stanley yelling to get the machine gun up there. I was the machine gunner but I don't remember hearing that, but I didn't need to be told. When looking for a place to set up the gun I saw a slight mound that Pineapple had found when he moved on-line with Pat, Ketch, and Danny. I carried the gun there, set it up and snapped the first 100 rounds to the leader I carried in the gun. Gary was on my immediate left. Pineapple was on my right. I couldn't see any target, but fired off two good bursts across the general area where I thought the shots had come from. Apparently, that got the enemy's attention. When I eased off the trigger, I heard Pineapple say "look for muzzle flashes." As I was looking, I suddenly felt a major thump on my arm, and heard myself let out a single extended bawl like a calf calling for its mother.

> This was the first of multiple wounds Ketch suffered in Vietnam; the last one was nearly fatal.

I was spun from my prone position. Lying on my right side, I looked down at my arm and saw a hole with red in it. My left wrist wouldn't move, making my arm almost useless. I heard someone else screeching in pain and realized it was Danny Smith.

I retrieved a bandage I carried in my first-aid pouch, but couldn't tie it. Pineapple quickly helped and told me to get back out of the way since I couldn't operate the gun anymore. I moved a short distance, but Pineapple screamed, "Not there. Get up and move back more." I did as told and lay down again. I heard the machine gun roaring. As Gary told me years later, "I just got on that trigger and let it go. Tyack took over as the assistant and kept belts of ammo attached. At some point, he tapped Gary on the helmet and shouted, 'Don't do that.' You'll burn it up."[8] A second machine gun was brought up and joined in the firing.

When Jerry, who had been walking drag, saw Danny get shot, he took Danny's grenade launcher and fired in the basic direction of the enemy's position. The presumed target distance was so close that some of the shrapnel came back on us. He only fired a few rounds with the M79 before deciding that wasn't working. At our reunion, Jerry told me:

> When I dove for cover, one of the lenses in my glasses got knocked out. Out of my one good eye, I could see everyone lying prone. Except David Stanley. He was kneeling and firing. Then a bullet hit his helmet and knocked him backwards. In like 10 to 15 seconds I saw three people get shot—you, Danny, and David."

---

8   Gary had been firing constantly instead of using bursts. Fortunately, the barrel did not overheat enough to warp. A critical responsibility of the machine gunner is to maintain it so when it's really needed, it works. I am proud to say my gun performed well that day.

After Pineapple helped me, he went to help Danny and then Ketch. Ketch resumed fire with his M16 from behind a 2-inch tree that offered no cover. He still couldn't see a specific target. The point man, Pat Toon, in shock made his way back to our location without his M16. Later, his pack would be found with multiple bullet holes in it.

While lying behind the rest of the squad, I listened to the firing. During the lulls, I heard Dave "Tennessee" Justice yelling at his 3-3 squad to get up and move. One of Tennessee's men, Ed Nored (two months in the bush at that time), later wrote:

> When the enemy opened fire on 3-2 squad, we hit the ground. I instantly went through three magazines firing into the bush. I had taped two magazines together on my "16." I stopped firing after sticking the 4th magazine in. I strained to see anything in the damn jungle to shoot at. The noise level was incredible. You went from near dead silence to an explosion of gunfire and people yelling. Soon, standing above me was Tennessee, my squad leader yelling, "Get up and move forward." "Dirty Doug" Gorton was on the ground ahead of me. I was looking at "Tennessee's" face and could hear him quite well. But I could not move. A fear took over me and paralyzed my body. I knew if I moved one inch the enemy would be able to see me and kill me. I was thinking everyone in the point squad is dead and now it's my turn. But everything changed when I saw Doug get up. I thought, "Doug don't get up. If you stay down, I can stay down." A childish thought to say the least. Seeing Doug get up meant only one thing—I had to get up. To this day it was the hardest thing I ever did. My body seemed to weigh a 1000 lbs. Then I spotted Tom Coker, his back to the enemy location, directing where we should spread out in front of the point squad. There was no cover to speak of, so we took to the ground, weapons ready and strained to see a target or movement ahead of us. But there was none to be seen.

> What I still remember most that day, and it is a personal thing that I don't think lasted more than a couple of minutes. It is a fear so deep you can't move. It's something that the Army can't duplicate in training. I was never so scared again as I was that day and will always be very happy I got up and followed Doug. But God it was hard. I will never forget it. Never.

Don Ketcham described the difficulty of finding the source of enemy fire in this ambush:

> When the shooting stopped, I counted the paces from where I had fired a full magazine of 16 out at the sound, it was 12 paces away yet I could not see the muzzle flash nor the doorway to the bunker. The bunker we had walked up on blended in with the background extremely well, the mound of the bunkers were tapered to the ground and small trees had been cut and jammed into the top surface of the bunkers. This made them meld right into the background—didn't even see it until the shooting was all done.

After the shooting subsided, I was still lying on the ground and people walked by in silence. I remember recognizing Oscar "Squirrel" Gaines. He had been in the squad, but left to join the Killer Team. Some in the squad tried to talk him out of it to no avail. Joining a small five or six person team who volunteered for high risk assignments was clearly brave but dangerous. Ironically, on December 9, I was the one lying wounded while Squirrel walked by in fine form. He didn't say anything, but as customary for him, his eyes bugged out when he recognized me. So it went in Vietnam.

LT. Mike Pickarski described what had happened during the ambush from his position with the 1st Platoon that had set up an ambush on the trail behind the 3rd Platoon.[9]

---

9 When we had set up camp on the night of December 8, I didn't know that the Commanding Officer had positioned Lt Piekarki's 1st platoon behind 3rd platoon to set up an ambush along the trail. When the enemy came back into the area we had vacated, they would themselves be ambushed and our rear would be protected.

We did an excellent job of covering 100-150 meters of this trail with Claymore mines. Before long, 3rd Platoon made contact with the enemy. About ten minutes into their contact, I looked to my left and saw three NVA soldiers moving slowly down the trail from my left to right. All of a sudden a guy behind a huge tree, stood up and started yelling "Gook! Gook!" Well shit, we blew the Claymores for what they were worth. The NVA turned and fired a B-40 (RPG) right into the clearing where I was watching them from. That was the end of the ambush. We hooked up with the rest of the company who, by this time had also broken contact. There were several wounded in 1st Platoon, as well as quite a few in 3rd Platoon, so we were pulled out of the boonies.

The eight wounded[10] were brought to a common point to wait for a Medevac. I sat next to someone I didn't recognize, presumably from 1st Platoon. It appeared he had lost an eye, probably from the aforementioned B-40 Rocket. I thought I'm glad that didn't happen to me. If the enemy we had faced had a B-40 Rocket, they likely would have used it on the machine gun, that is, me, Gary, and Pineapple.

Captain Cary Perkins came to speak to each of the wounded. He looked at my arm

> To Sergeant David Stanley who immediately rushed up to get on-line with the point squad and to Tennessee and his squad, thank you seems inadequate. Nonetheless, THANK YOU.

and said "Well, it is all over for you, you are going home." I just looked at him in stunned disbelief as if to say, "Well, how do you know?" He knew my limp and useless wrist would not be a quick fix. He told me to say my good-byes, as I would not be back.

Helicopters were able to land. Unusually, Ketch went out on a Light Observation Helicopter. I was in a Huey for a short ride to LZ Ellen. I remember being anxiously greeted along with the other wounded by Lt.

---

10 Arlyn Perkey, Marcel Gorre, Don Ketcham, and Dan Smith from the 3-2 squad; James Schmidt from 3-3 squad; David Stanley, 3rd Platoon Leader; Chris Partish and Charles Brown from 1st Platoon).

Wiggins. He called to me by name. He had been our Platoon Leader for a while. He was good; he cared about us.

From LZ Ellen, Ketch and I were probably on the same bird that went to an aid station where they X-rayed my arm. The technician marveled at the perfect conical shape of the bullet, indicating that it had not deflected from anything before hitting me. It was not lodged against the bone. It was lying in flesh. Why had it stopped there? An AK 47 round fired from that distance of 25 yards would normally go through an arm and in my case into my body cavity (close to the heart). I had my left hand on the M-60 stock to hold it down when fired.

All I can say is that I had two grandmothers leading other relatives and friends in prayer for me. I know people at my own Pleasant Hill United Methodist Church where my parents attended were praying in support of me. I have never forgotten that and still return to this small country church to worship when I can and maintain contact with old friends. I don't feel I survived because of my own Christian commitment at that time. It just wasn't my time to go. I remain ever grateful to God for sparing me and for the good life I have enjoyed since then. Whenever December 9 rolls around, I try to take it as a "be grateful that I am alive day." Was it a coincidence or a God-incidence? To me, it was a God-incidence.

We flew by Huey from the aid station to a hospital in Saigon. I hopped out and headed to the door thinking, "This looks mighty fine to me." A clear voice ordered me back on the Huey. Shucks! Ketch and I were separated when I was taken on to Long Binh.

At the hospital, I was placed on a bed, and a guy started to remove my boots. I said, "It might smell pretty bad when you take those off." He never looked up or said a word. I suspected he didn't have any trouble smelling me with the boots still on. Before they administered anesthesia for surgery, I asked if they would save the bullet as a memento. They said yes, but when I asked for it the next day it was long gone. I woke from surgery about 7:30 p.m. and was taken back to a ward with bed after bed of patients. I didn't have my glasses and couldn't see much. It didn't matter. I wasn't feeling very sociable.

The doctors told me the bullet hit a nerve making me unable to raise my limp wrist. I had heard of a radial nerve before, but I was about to learn much, much more.

December 10. In the morning, I retrieved my glasses and other belongings that had been on me when I was shot. I had not shaved for about nine days so I looked like hell and probably smelled worse. Out in the boonies, everyone had body odor and didn't worry about it. Here, where everyone was clean, I became conscious of my appearance. A guy in charge of the ward told me nicely to go shave and shower, which I gladly did. What a shock I encountered. There were about six guys in the bathroom doing their treatment for VD. Being from rural Iowa, I had never seen anything like that.

When I returned to the ward, a Vietnamese guy was curious that I had among my personal things one unfired AK47 round and one empty AK47 shell case. I tried to explain that I carried those two AK47 rounds (fired and unfired) to remind me to remain ever cautious.

December 11. Someone came to ask whether I wanted my parents to be notified regarding my wound or if I wanted to send them a letter. I chose to write and was told, "Write to them now."

December 12. In the morning, someone called for me to get my things and be ready to leave for Japan. The word was, if they sent you to Japan, you would not come back to Vietnam. Captain Perkins had been correct. It was over for me.

> Back in Iowa, my mother opened the mailbox and knew immediately that something was wrong. "The stationery was different," she told me later. "But I knew you must be alive because it was your handwriting."

LOOKING BACK

In a phone conversation, Pineapple told me he lamented going up that hill on December 9. I reminded him it wasn't his decision. Back then, the squad had no idea where we were in relation to the surrounding topography. The NVA bunker complex, now encircled by our defensive perimeter, was on the inside of a curve in the Song Be. We were only about 200 meters from the river's edge. That blocked us from leaving the area on foot to the north or west. They probably had an ambush prepared for us no matter how we went. Up the hill was probably as good (or bad) as any other direction.

As a machine gunner, I always tried to be aware of my squad members' whereabouts. Although I had been wounded, I was conscious and thought I had an accurate understanding of my situation and the surrounding action. During a reunion 48 years later, Gary Borkowski and Jerry Reeves fleshed out the scene with details I didn't remember.

Gary told me that when he got behind the gun, only one leg was locked down. I always carried the gun on my shoulder, holding onto one leg locked in the down position. In my haste to start firing, I may have failed to securely lock down the second leg. I know I fired across a fairly wide area, because I didn't know precisely where the NVA were. Gary also said I was no longer lying behind the gun and there was blood on my face. I had always thought that Jerry was on my left, but he and David Stanley had moved up on line on my right.

My misperception of these details underscores how the adrenalin rush in the heat of battle can distort impressions. I was mindful of this possibility as I interviewed those who had "witnessed" Don's ambush.

In talking with Gary, I had always assumed that being that close was unnerving for him. He revealed how depressed he had been the night of December 9, when the day's events convinced him he was never going to make it back alive. Jim Brinker's book, *West of Hue,* relates how many grunts had this type of turning point during their tour.

> Gary completed his full year in the boonies and now lives in Carroll, Iowa.

CHAPTER 6

CAPTURE

> As described in "An Eye for an Eye," many skirmishes were retaliatory. Our forces attacked NVA units; NVA units attacked ours. Given the events of June 17, 1969, it seems likely that Don Sparks' squad was caught in such a retaliatory incident.

SEARCHING FOR THE PUZZLE PIECES

SOME OF THE FACTS SURROUNDING the June 17 ambush of Don Sparks' squad are difficult to pin down. Contradictory statements, inaccurate information in official records, and discrepancies in the memories of those present during and after the ambush create an aura of mystery. There is undoubtedly more to the story than I have described below; I didn't find all the pieces of the puzzle and do not claim to represent every perspective. As I pieced together the following account, the thing most glaring was communication failure. What follows has been gleaned from after-the-fact sources including telephone interviews I conducted and C Company's entries in the Duty Officer's Log. I gave high credence to recent oral statements from active participants. Some old records I examined were of highly questionable validity, and were largely discounted. What has emerged is a picture of a tragic ambush, narrowly missed opportunities for rescuing Don, and a chain of decisions that resulted in his designation as MIA, POW (not recovered), and finally, Last Known Alive.

BACKGROUND

On May 14, 1969 at the Battle for Nui Yon Hill, C Company lost a number of experienced soldiers. Although some WIA eventually rejoined the company in the field, most were still in the rear recovering when Don Sparks and other "Cherries" joined C Company at the beginning of June.

Don Sparks, Al Shaw, and Marvin Timperley had completed in-country training together in Chu Lai and were assigned to Joel Pasternack's Squad. Fellow squad

> **KEY PERSONNEL IN DON SPARKS' SQUAD**
>
> Joel Pasternack, Squad Leader
>
> **SQUAD MEMBERS**
> Larry Graham
> Don Hull
> Al Shaw
> Don Sparks
> Marvin Timperley

members Larry Graham and Don Hull had only a little more time in country than Cherries Don, Al, and Marvin.

Don's squad was part of C Company's 1st Platoon under the leadership of Acting Platoon Sergeant PFC David Classick.[11] PFC Classic had been a Specialist 4th Class, with in-country ranger training, but had been demoted to PFC because of a marijuana incident. On the fateful day of June 17, no officer was present in the 1st Platoon.

Squad leader Joel Pasternack, as a survivor of the Battle for Nui Yon Hill, was combat experienced. However, he had lost his good

---

11 See Appendix 2c for an overview of chain-of-command for Don on June 17, 1969.

friend, PFC William Daniels, in that battle and as a result, remained emotionally distant from the new men in his squad. He had adopted the survival mentality of "if I don't know you, it won't hurt so bad when you are gone." Even so, he positively remembers Don as the new guy from Iowa who had the outstanding knack of digging a nice, neat, precise fox hole. He also told me, "Don was integrating into the squad very well."

According to C Company Executive Officer Jim Gordon, Don's squad was operating in a free fire zone, meaning that civilians were not allowed in the area. Nevertheless, old men, women and children—seemingly innocent civilians—were often encountered and created an enormous quandary for GIs. Women and children, who would wave and accept little gifts (e.g., candy, gum, C-rations, cigarettes) from Americans, were often friends and relatives of Viet Cong forces. In rural areas controlled by the enemy, anyone helping Americans would not be safe; they were a terrorized population. So even if the civilians knew our men were headed into harm's way, they would give no warning. This led to some soldier's unfavorable response to probable civilians. Squad-mate Marvin remembers Don as a very nice guy who in the short time they were together showed no tolerance for bad treatment of obvious non-combatants.

On June 16, Don wrote the following in a letter home:

> There is definitely a lot of static close to where we are. We have been pulling guard duty on one of the firebases the past week. Now they choppered us out to join A Company. After they run airstrikes and artillery they move us into the area.

The area to which Don was referring was the Village of Phuoc Son (now Tien Son) in Tien Phuoc District, southeast of LZ Center. Forward Observer Charles Miller said this was not an area they normally operated in. Map 3 provides an overview of the locations referenced in the following account of the ambush events of June 17, 1969.

MAP 3
LOCATION OF DONALD SPARKS CAPTURE

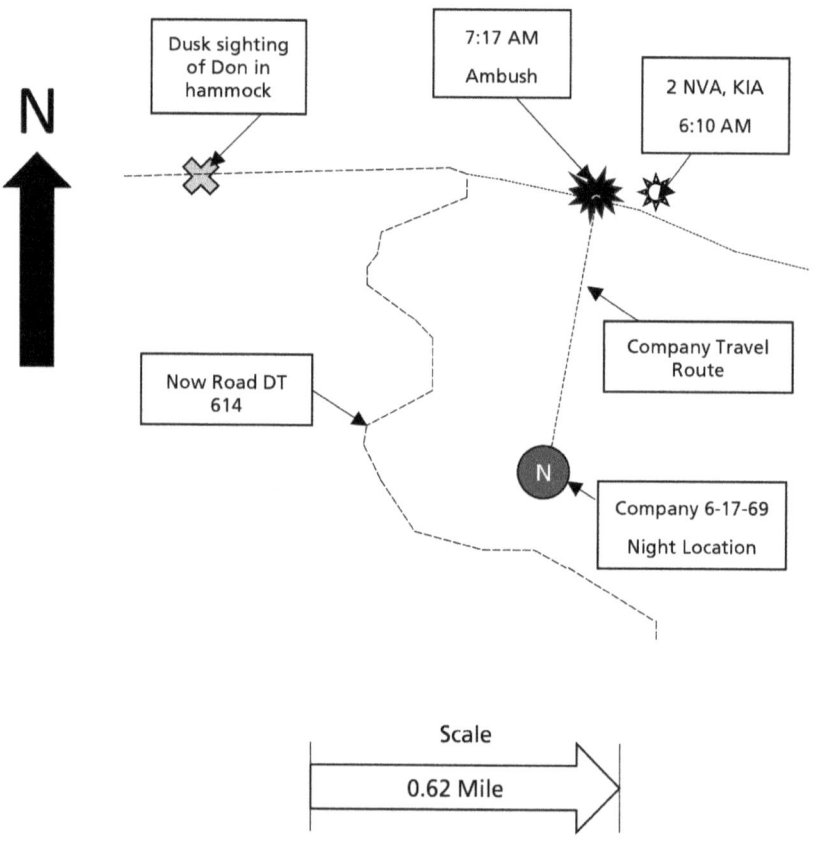

On the morning of June 17, 1969, Company C left their night location, moving northeast in a single file. A fleeing woodcutter was observed. The point squad followed while the remainder of the company waited. The squad was ambushed. Point man Larry Graham was killed. Don Sparks was wounded and captured.

Chapter 6

This is Larry Graham going through the process of being sent to Vietnam. His sleeping quarters would be soon be much less comfortable.

PHOTOGRAPH COURTESY OF LARRY GRAHAM'S FAMILY

Troops were flown to Vietnam on chartered planes. Larry waves good-bye to loved ones in The World. The next day it would be GOOD MORNING VIETNAM. He would soon be followed by Don Sparks. About 1 month later, I would experience the same regimen.

PHOTOGRAPH COURTESY OF LARRY GRAHAM'S FAMILY

*Larry Graham took this picture of a rice farmer.
This thatched hooch is similar to the one Larry and
Don were circling when they were ambushed.*

PHOTOGRAPH COURTESY OF LARRY GRAHAM'S FAMILY

*Don was probably nearby when Larry Graham took this picture
of a mama san outside her thatch-roof hooch. She may have had
relatives who were Viet Cong, and Don probably never imagined
he would soon be held captive by such innocent looking people.*

PHOTOGRAPH COURTESY OF LARRY GRAHAM'S FAMILY

Chapter 6

*Joel Pasternack was Don and Larry's squad leader on June 17, 1969.
He is the last known American to have seen Don Sparks alive.*
PHOTOGRAPH COURTESY OF LARRY GRAHAM'S FAMILY

*Larry Graham holding an M-79 Grenade Launcher that
could fire individual grenades or rounds of buckshot.*
PHOTOGRAPH COURTESY OF LARRY GRAHAM'S FAMILY

Larry Graham relaxes and reads while keeping his M-16 within easy reach. Larry was carrying an M-16 on the day he was killed.

PHOTOGRAPH COURTESY OF LARRY GRAHAM'S FAMILY

AMBUSH

June 17. 5:16 a.m. The sun rose on the night laager of Don's squad. The Duty Officer's Log entry at 6:10 a.m. indicated that a unit of C Company had engaged five NVA sometime the previous evening or earlier that morning. Two of the five NVA were killed;[12] the other three escaped.[13]

With Joel's squad in the lead, C Company headed northeast from their night laager. Walking single-file, Larry was on point, followed by Don Sparks, Joel, Don Hull (carrying the radio), Al, and Marvin. A Vietnamese papa san wood cutter ahead on the right ran away as they approached. Larry Graham and Don Sparks started to run after him. Joel stopped them and said "hey, we don't do that." Meaning, not to follow him. Joel knew it was very dangerous to follow a departing potential enemy. At this point, David Classick joined the group and ordered them to pursue the papa san. Joel did not want to, telling the men he thought he had a good enough relationship with Company Commander (CO) Ernie Carrier that he was willing to challenge Classick's order. However, the squad members said they were willing to go—a courageous though not prudent choice. They dropped their heavies, and since Marvin had previously been walking point, Joel assigned him the safer task of guarding the packs. The other five squad members moved forward toward the departing wood cutter, in the general direction they had already been going. The remainder of 1st Platoon and all of 2nd Platoon remained behind.

7:17 a.m. Don's squad climbed a steep incline toward a three-sided, straw-covered hooch supported on bamboo stilts.[14] The squad approached the hooch with Larry and Don Sparks in front, followed by Joel, Don Hull, and Al. Suddenly, as Larry and Don rounded the hooch corner, a 30-caliber machine gun opened fire through the straw-covered

---

12 U.S. soldiers recovered the NVA AK-47s and noted the serial numbers for the weapons; thereby verifying that these were actual kills, not inflated body counts.

13 I was unable to find anyone who recalled the event. I suspect 3rd Platoon was deployed separately from the rest of the company on a night ambush. Joel Pasternack is certain he was never advised that his squad would be moving close to where this reported event had occurred.

14 Joel remembers how strange it was for this single, isolated hooch to be in such a dense jungle nowhere near any water source. In hindsight, Joel wonders if the wood cutter may have been a decoy to lead them into the ambush.

walls. Larry managed to discharge a few rounds. Joel saw Larry and Don get spun into the air, hitting the ground when the burst of gunfire stopped. He felt certain both Larry and Don had to be dead. Joel never saw how many NVA were there and speculates the enemy may not have actually seen Larry and Don, but targeted the sound of their footsteps.

When Larry and Don were hit, Joel, Don Hull, and Al literally fell back down the very steep slope. Joel described it as low-crawling backwards. Joel ended up in the area occupied by the 2nd platoon. CO Carrier was there and asked "what the hell happened?" He was livid.

SSGT Fred Salerno and men from the 2nd Platoon were ordered to approach the ambush site. During a telephone interview, Fred told me, "We got close enough to hear an American screaming." (Presumably that was Don Sparks.) "Before we could reach him, the point man was

---

IDENTITY OF 2ND PLATOON POINT MAN

The identity of the point man who lost his life trying to reach Don is unknown.

Interviews with Fred Salerno and Jim "Doc" McCloughan (head company medic) point to a likely mix-up in the identification of this deceased point man. The Vietnam Veterans Memorial Wall shows a medic, David Loew from 3/21st headquarters, as KIA on the 17th. Fred and Doc both assured me that is not the correct name. The man killed was not a medic, and David Loew was not with the company. Unfortunately, neither they nor anyone else from 2nd Platoon I have interviewed can remember this point man's name. This suggests he had not been with the company a long time.

Don's last letter home indicates, Company A was operating in the same area. The Virtual Wall shows an Anthony H. Figueroa, Jr., with Company A, as being killed on June 19, 1969. It is plausible that Loew was with Co. A, and was killed on the 19th, while Figueroa was with Co. C and was killed on the 17th. At the time of this writing, this remains one of the unsolved mysteries of this whole sad event. I reached Anthony Figueroa's family to explore the probability that Anthony was the deceased point man. His identity has not been confirmed.

shot in the head and killed instantly."[15] It is not known if this was before or after the airstrike described below.

In the immediate aftermath of the ambush, conflicting accounts of Larry's and Don's fate may have been relayed up the chain of command. Somewhere along the line, however, the view that both men were dead prevailed.

Joel remembers that CO Ernie Carrier called in an airstrike. Joel and others were about 1000 meters away when the bombs dropped on the ambush site. Although a spotter plane would normally accompany the jet bombers, Joel does not specifically remember seeing one. Nor was he sure whether Air Force or Navy jets dropped the 250-pound bombs. The 2nd platoon contingent were the only C Company personnel with first-hand knowledge that at least one soldier was alive. It is not known why this information did not reach, was not believed, or was not acted upon by CO Carrier; a vital communication failure.

At 2:30 p.m. another NVA with no weapon or military equipment was reported killed in the vicinity of the 6:10 a.m. fire fight. This indicates that by mid-afternoon a unit of C Company was back in the general area to the east of where Donny and Larry had been shot. By the end of the day, Larry Graham and Don Sparks were officially listed as MIA. Those in Don's squad and at the command post thought both were KIA.[16] For Larry Graham this was correct. But not so for Don Sparks—a reality more evident on the morning of June 18.

June 18. At 8:10 a.m., C Company returned to the site of the previous day's ambush and recovered Larry Graham's body. Don Sparks was not found, alive or dead. However, Don's boot with a dog tag attached

---

15 I wanted to interview any of the other men who accompanied Fred that day in order to learn what they remembered. Unfortunately, my efforts to contact them failed.
16 When I contacted people 46 years later, the only people with memory of the incident were those personally involved in 1st or 2nd platoon. For example, John Guccione, the company Radio Telephone Operator at the time, was shocked when I told him what happened to Don. He had no idea they had lost a man as a POW. This suggests the command post did not receive word of the American screams heard by the 2nd Platoon contingent or did not consider it credible. While Company Commander Ernie Carrier indicated he had no memory of this incident, he had suffered a stroke, and his memory may have been impaired. He passed away May 20, 2018.

to the laces was found.[17] I can imagine the anguish experienced by those who realized a comrade—perhaps alive—had been left behind. At that point, it may have been easier to deny the evidence of Don's surviving the ambush and maintain the belief he was dead. Perhaps that made their anguish more bearable. Unfortunately, for Don, denial was impossible. He was alive, seriously wounded, isolated, and at the mercy of an enemy whose language he could not comprehend.

AFTER THE AMBUSH

What happened to Don after the ambush has been gleaned from post-war interviews with Vietnamese personnel. In 2011, Le Ngoc Do[18] said he had spotted an American waving his shirt trying to get the attention of American aircraft.[19] Unfortunately, Don's attempts to flag down help attracted Le Ngoc Do's attention, who, as part of a reconnaissance team, may have been one of the three NVA who had escaped the ambush recorded in the Duty Officers Log at 6:10 a.m. The precise time of Don's capture is not known, but it was probably sometime after the 2nd Platoon approached the ambush site, heard an American screaming, and retreated with their KIA-point man. That man was evacuated in the 10:20 a.m. dust off of WIA-PFC Acting Platoon Sergeant David Classick. It is not known who became Acting 1st Platoon Sergeant after his departure.

According to a Mr. Nguyen Cu, Don was unable to walk. He was carried in a hammock to a hooch located about 200 meters northeast of the ambush site. About 30 minutes later, he was evacuated westward.

---

17 Some grunts carried one dog tag on a chain around their neck, and one in the lace of their boot. Apparently, that is what Don had done. Both Marvin Timperley and Al Shaw remember seeing it, but don't know who found it or what was done with it. I never found firm evidence that anyone from the command post ever learned of the recovered empty boot with Don's dog tag. Both Joel Pasternack and Executive Office Jim Gordon indicated they had never heard of this boot and dog tag. Joel added that he never returned to the ambush site. Likewise, Joel and Jim both indicated they were never told of an American heard screaming.
18 Le was the former Political Officer 21st Reconnaissance Company, 31st Regiment, PAVN 2nd Division.
19 No record is available to indicate whether Don was waving at a helicopter or a spotter plane that had been called in prior to the air strike. Nor is there evidence that an air search for Don had been conducted. This lends credence to the belief that Don was already presumed dead.

Based on the location of the following account by villager Nguyen Ngoc Anh, it is likely that Don was being taken to a nearby aid station.

According to Mr. Nguyen Anh, he briefly encountered four NVA soldiers carrying an American in a hammock. The soldiers told him the prisoner had been wounded in the leg and captured at a battle at Phuoc Son Village. Mr. Anh thought he was the only one who saw the men since he never heard anyone else in the village discussing it. At the time of this evening sighting (presumably on the 17th), Don's company was likely at their night location less than a mile away.

> The thought of my wounded, crippled friend swaying back and forth in a hammock as four enemy soldiers took him away is almost more than I can wrap my mind around. Did they give him anything for pain? How far did they go that night? What fear must have gripped him? I imagine him praying like he never prayed before; his thoughts on home and wondering if he would ever see family and friends again. As a Prisoner of War (POW) Don would never again talk to another American, eat Mom's fried chicken with mashed potatoes and gravy, drive a John Deere tractor across the field, or dance at the Star Line Ballroom in Carroll, Iowa. I wonder if he was re-thinking his departing comment to Jim Brinker, "Well this will be an adventure and I have myself ready."

On an unrecalled date, Mr. Chau Khac Tao[20], Mr. Niem, and one soldier observed two U.S. helicopters circling Tranh Hill, apparently searching for something or someone. The three Vietnamese used binoculars to survey the area and saw an American soldier repeatedly standing and sitting. Apparently, the helicopters never saw this and departed the area. Mr. Tao and his comrades then captured the American, who had serious wounds to his right thigh and heel. It became clear to Mr. Tao that the soldier had been doing a stand and sit motion to signal the helicopters. However, because of his leg wounds, he was unable to stand for long. Mr. Tao and his comrades carried the American soldier

---

20 Mr. Chau Khac Tao, 31st Regimental Commander's aide.

to the 31st Regimental Headquarters. Members of the Regimental Transportation Team took him to the CK120 Field Hospital. Mr. Tao's physical description of the American soldier's injuries is consistent with other witnesses' descriptions of Don Sparks' wounds.

Considering the distance of the 31st Regimental Headquarters from the capture site, I surmise this incident occurred on June 18 or 19. We don't know if the helicopters were incidentally in the area, or if they were part of a search initiated after Don Sparks' body was not found alongside Larry Graham at the capture site. If there was an aerial search, it was most likely initiated then. I suspect this was Don's first escape attempt. His ability to stand at all suggests his wounds were not yet infected. It is difficult not to wonder "what if!" If the observers in the helicopters would have seen and recognized him, Don's fate might have been different. We will never know how close he came to rescue at this early stage of captivity.

In February 1971, a former guerilla rallier told of seeing an American POW held by four NVA guards armed with AK-47s at Phuoc Ha Village (now Tien Ha) on the southern bank of the Song Chang. This is about 4.5 miles (air distance) from the capture site. The POW had bandaged leg wounds and was conversing in English with a VC doctor. He had been carried there by NVA soldiers after he was wounded and captured by the 31st Regiment at Phuoc Son Village.[21] The American was dressed in green pants, blue shirt, and was not wearing shoes. The green pants were probably Don's fatigue pants. The blue shirt had to be provided by the Vietnamese. They probably didn't want their prisoner to go into shock. Being barefoot is consistent with one boot damaged in the ambush and the other one removed and left at the site. Another observation (presumably later) indicates his dress was changed to blue pajamas and later black pajamas and tire sandals. This makes sense since they would not want his appearance in Army fatigues to make him more recognizable from a distance.

In November 1971, an NVA rallier stated that while he was in the 31st Regiment they had engaged an element of the 196th Light Infantry Brigade (Don's Brigade) and he saw a U.S. POW who was wounded in the thigh and was evacuated to the 31st Regimental Headquarters. Forty years later, in 2011, this observation was supported by Mr. Hoang

---

21 Phuoc Son has been renamed Tien Son. That is the name currently used on Google Earth.

Minh Tien, former commander of the 17th Company, 31st Regiment. He said an American prisoner matching Don's description was brought to the 31st Headquarters. This location is about 6 miles (air distance) from the capture site. Members of the Recon team, including Le Ngoc Do (Don's initial captor), escorted him away.

Many Americans may find it surprising that the North Vietnamese would expend so much effort to carry a crippled enemy prisoner for miles in a hammock. These were, however, people accustomed to hard physical work and limited mechanized transportation. Carrying 170 lbs. was not unusual. Still, it was a lot of effort for people with very limited resources. It is less likely they were motivated by kindness than by the value of an American prisoner as propaganda. It demonstrated to the populace that Vietnamese communist forces controlled the area. Even with all of the American's flying machines and bombs, they could not keep the PAVN from toting this man through the countryside in a hammock.

THE OFFICIAL U.S. MILITARY INQUIRY

On June 26, 1969, a three-member Board of Inquiry was convened at LZ Center. The Board comprised Battalion Executive Officer Roger B Olson (chair), Company C Executive Officer Jim V. Gordon, and Company A Executive Officer James Shoesmith. Statements purportedly made on June 23, 1969 by Joel Pasternack, David Classick, and Fred Salerno, all stated with confidence that both Don and Larry were dead, describing specific wounds on the bodies. We now know those statements were incorrect.

The Duty Officer's Log shows the company's night location remained the same from June 17 to June 21, 1969. In talking with me, Jim Gordon confirmed that it was very unusual for an infantry company to remain in a single night laager for that long. Jim thought they must have stayed in the area to continue the search for evidence of Don and because of frequent contact with the enemy. The Board of Inquiry indicated the Battalion Commander visited the incident site on June 21, 1969. It is probable C Company remained in the area to be available for the Battalion Commander's on-site inspection. This was an indication he was trying to sort out in his own mind what had happened. Jim Gordon was uncertain who the Battalion Commander was at that time, because there had been a transition from Andrew Brandenburg to Eli Howard in June of 1969. Eli Howard was killed in a helicopter crash on August 19, 1969 and so could offer no additional information about the events in question. I was unable to contact Andrew Brandenburg.

At the conclusion of its inquiry, the Board's official statement was:

It is the board's recommendation that PFC Sparks, Donald L., U.S.56547065, status be changed from missing in action to killed in action, body not recovered.

Major General Lloyd B. Ramsey, however, disagreed with the Board's recommendation to declare Don KIA. He personally signed the following statement regarding the recommendation of the June 26, 1969, Board of Inquiry:

Since PFC Sparks was not recovered and according to board witness statements not physically examined for pulse count, signs of life, etc., the possibility exists, though remote, that PFC Sparks could have been alive when last seen by board witnesses.

The board recommendation that status of PFC Sparks be changed from "missing in action" to killed in action, body not recovered" is disapproved, and it is recommended that status of PFC Sparks be continued as "missing in action."

Fortunately, the General's recommendation was accepted, and Don's MIA status was maintained. We will never know if he believed the incorrect statements and it really was a close call for him, or if that was just a nice way to say, "No, I don't believe this." In any case, we are grateful. I believe if Don had been declared KIA at that time, it would have been much more difficult to get the Department of Defense to overturn that finding and consider Don a POW to be investigated as a high priority, Last Known Alive case.

> On March 17, 1970, General Ramsey's helicopter crashed in enemy held territory. Two men were killed and General Ramsey was seriously injured. Eighteen hours later, Ramsey and the other survivors were rescued. The General's combat career was over.
>
> I wanted to contact General Ramsey to let him know he made the correct decision regarding Don's MIA status. Unfortunately, I was too late; he had passed away February 23, 2016, in Roanoke, VA at the age of 97. It is doubtful I would have been able to get through the privacy protection barrier, but it would have been worth a try.

On July 5, 1969, General William C. Westmoreland's Office sent what appears to be a form letter from the General, United States Army, Chief of Staff, to Don's parents. Westmoreland's printed name was stamped in the signature block. Following is an excerpt from the letter:

> *Extensive and continuous aerial and ground searches are being conducted and leaflets have been dropped announcing the offer of rewards for the recovery of missing personnel. As soon as any additional information is received, the Adjutant General will pass it on to you without delay.*

While the letter contains words intended to reassure, the stamped name lacked a personal touch. By that time, Westmoreland's name was already associated with bloated enemy body counts intended to reassure the President and the American public that the War was being won. Calvin and Arloha Sparks would later discover the hollowness of Westmoreland's promise regarding any additional information. This was an early bureaucratic response from a high office far removed from the scene with no valid sense of what was or was not being done.

I found no evidence of any search activity beyond June 21, 1969, until August 29, 1969, when then Company Commander Jim Gordon, returned to the night laager used from June 17 to June 21. When Jim and his men returned to the incident site, the party only included a couple of men who had been there in June. At the ambush site, they found bomb craters from the air strike, but nothing else.

POSTSCRIPT

As I worked to understand not only what happened to Don, but why, I couldn't help but think about the differences between my ambush experience and Don's. I was in an eight-man squad as compared to the five-man contingent of Don's squad. My squad had a seasoned leader and most of the rest of us had been in the bush for at least a few months. Don's squad was also led by an experienced leader, but the remainder of the squad consisted of four "Cherries." We were working our way up a slight inclined slope and were armed with a machine gun. Don's squad was located at the edge of a steep drop-off which made maneuvering difficult. They had been led into a very disadvantageous position. When enemy fire temporarily put one of our men down and the follow-up blast took two more men out of commission, the Platoon Leader immediately moved forward, followed by an additional machine gun and backup squad. We were able to respond with significant fire power. When two members of Don's squad were taken out when the enemy opened fire with a machine gun, the three remaining men had no machine gun and any potential back-up was a considerable distance behind.

Admittedly, in the ambush I experienced our return fire was not well directed as none of us ever had a specific visible target. We fired in the general direction of the sound of the enemy fire. Nonetheless, it was enough to convince the enemy that even with their advantageous bunker positions, they didn't want to remain very long in the fight. We never gave up control of the ground where our wounded lay. While being ambushed was never a desirable situation, the lack of adequate and immediate backup firepower contributed significantly to the disastrous results for Larry and Don.

CHAPTER 7

HOSPITAL

BACKGROUND

UPON MY EVACUATION FROM JAPAN, I was treated at Fitzsimmons Army Hospital, a medical campus located on several acres in Aurora, Colorado, a suburb of Denver. Again, the contrast between my situation and Don's was starkly bleak. My wounds were treated in sterile operating and recovery rooms. Bandages were changed; medications were available; good, safe, healthy food was served at every meal. I could easily communicate my needs to my care givers. One night patients were even entertained by Gladys Knight and the Pips followed by Bobbi Gentry.

Quite a different picture is painted by information pieced together from interviews with former staff at the Vietnamese hospital where Don was treated and held captive. Not surprisingly, I found a number of inconsistencies in these eye-witness reports—variations due to the passage of time and possibly the translation from Vietnamese to English. In one case, a staff person was interviewed jointly with the individual who had been the political officer for the hospital. As a result, she may have been somewhat circumspect in her comments. Nevertheless, details provided by these personnel support the conclusion that Don was wounded, not killed, in action and subsequently held as a POW. Further, a fairly accurate picture of Don's final months does emerge from this patchwork of information.

Located in the mountains west of the Song Tranh was GK38, a parent medical facility with four subsidiary field hospitals—CK110, CK120, CK130, and CK140. CK120 was not a single stationary hospital campus, but a series of mobile facilities above and below ground in the general vicinity of Thon Bon Hamlets 1-6. Mr. Doan Huu Nghi, a political officer at CK120 described it as being located at Thon Bon 5, in Tien Lanh Village situated east of the Song Tranh and about eleven air miles from the site where Don had been captured. *(See Map 4)*[22]

From the air, the CK120 complex would not stand out from other structures in Tien Lanh Village. However, in August 1968, the hamlets in the surrounding area had been bombed by U.S. forces in preparation for an infantry assault by the 3rd Platoon, C Company, 5th/46th. After the bombing ended, two Chinook helicopters brought in troops. Fortunately, most of the Vietnamese defending the area had scattered. As was the case with the mobile facilities, patients were moved as the NVA troops evacuated the area. David Taylor, author of *Our War*, and Joe Scurlock, a medic with the 3rd Platoon, offered this description of the area.

> CK120 was situated in a sparsely populated valley about a mile wide. A mud road, gutted with holes and ditches traversed the valley. When the 3rd Platoon entered the area, they found an extensive network of tunnels housing operating and recovery rooms supplied with scissors, forceps, surgical gloves and medicines such as penicillin, sleeping tablets, aspirin,

---

[22] In recent years, this area has received some notice in the scientific community as a place where the few remaining wild Asian Elephants have come into conflict with the growing human population, causing crop and building damage. They were probably an issue when Don was there. With Don's interest in agricultural I am sure he observed crops grown in the area However, he faced far bigger problems. In no way was this anything like his agricultural tour of Europe.

and dysentery tablets. Fresh, blood-stained bedding indicated the facility had been vacated recently.

Soldiers searching the area found 20 graves, five of which had been freshly dug. Bones were strewn about, evidence of amputations. Joe Scurlock evacuated two emaciated women who were suffering either from malaria or having blood drained for transfusions.[23] Each weighed less than 50 lbs. When the dust-off arrived, the women clung to Scurlock. "You could tell they felt secure with and didn't want to let go."

---

23 With blood in short supply for the treatment of soldiers, Vietnamese civilians were often used as "donors." It was not unusual for blood to be taken from civilians more frequently than was safe. There is a suggestion that Don's blood may also have been drawn for this purpose as he recovered from his wounds (see Mrs. Pham statement below).

MAP 4
LOCATION OF CK 120 HOSPITAL
Tien Lanh Village / Thon bon Hamlets Area

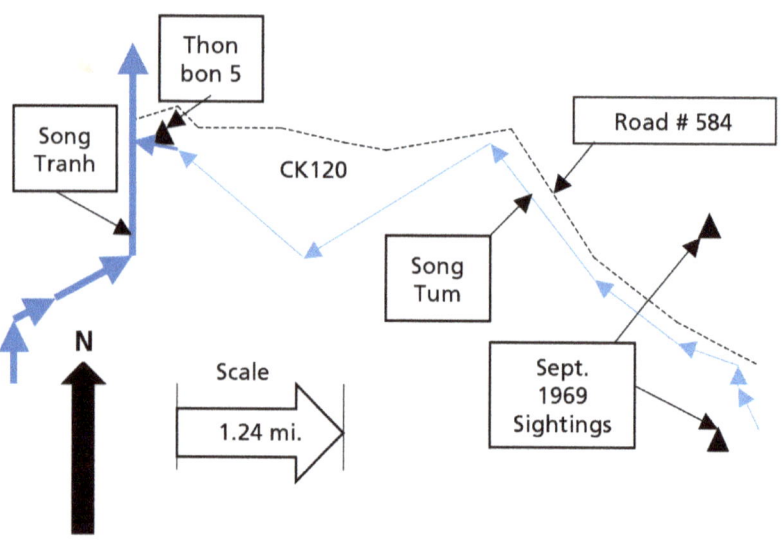

The CK 120 Hospital was mobile and located in spaces above and below ground along a road identified in 1970 with the number 584. On Google Earth, it is now identified as Lanh Ngoc Hiep. Don was brought to this general area after he was captured and held here until February of 1970. He was then taken south along the Song Tranh to where he was last seen at Cau Chim Crossroads.

Chapter 7

DON'S ARRIVAL AT FIELD HOSPITAL CK120

CK120 had one doctor, two medical officers, and a staff of forty people who treated as many as 150 North Vietnamese Army/Viet Cong (NVA/VC) patients. The exact date of Don's arrival at the mobile hospital is not known. However, sources indicate he was held there for eight months from July 1969 to February 1970. Multiple witnesses of Don's arrival described a wound in his right thigh or buttocks and a foot wound where his heel had been shot off. It seems Don's right thigh wound had been treated at a North Vietnamese aid station. Former medic Le Thanh Liem said he was the first to treat "Spoc" after his arrival at CK120. Mr. Liem initially repaired Don's shattered right ankle. Three days later, he removed a bullet from Don's thigh, because it had begun to swell. The wounds became infected causing considerable delay in his recovery.

Mr. Liem said Don was the only American he treated during the ten years he served at CK120. He learned Don's name from Don himself. How that came about provides a glimpse into life for a lone POW in rural South Vietnam. The Tien Lanh Village was located in an area controlled by the Region 5 Communist Party Committee. The Committee had what they referred to as a Proselytizing Section that contained Proselytizing Personnel or Proselytizing Cadre whose job was to convert POWs to the side of communist forces. Testimony from returning American POWs provide evidence that conversion techniques were often painful (torturous). A Proselytizing Cadre came to CK120, and Don had to make a written statement. Don showed Mr. Liem the statement and pointed to his name.

Mr. Thanh Van Ky had been wounded in 1965 while serving in a VC military unit. He was sent to CK120 to recover, but was never again suitable for regular service. Until the end of the war, he remained at the hospital where he provided food for the staff and patients. Mr. Ky knew Don Sparks' name because he saw a letter written in December 1969 when Don asked his family to send him a Christmas gift. Mr. Ky could not read English, but an interpreter (probably proselytizing cadre) explained the content of the letter to him.

Mr. Ky was responsible for Don's diet. There were three different diets that could be provided to the hospital staff and patients depending on their physical condition. These were called Cham (injured), Chung (common), and Binh (ill). At first, Don was unable to eat the rice or rice noodles that were the normal diet of the hospital staff and patients. The staff bought some beef and cut it into small pieces to give to him. When he ate, he started to recover. Don always received the highest-level rations, which included a lot of corn. Don was very nervous when he first arrived at the hospital, but after receiving medical treatment and food his anxiety lessened.

Mrs. Hoang Thi Pham, a medic at CK120, said that when a blue-pajama clad American arrived at the hospital he was conscious. He had no uniform, no boots, no dog tags or other personal effects. He had a right thigh/buttock wound and his entire right heel was missing. The tip of one finger was missing, but that was from an old injury. Mrs. Pham was responsible for feeding the American, washing and bandaging his wounds, and giving him medications when they were available. She said he was not allergic to penicillin and that he had type "A" blood, because the American was used for blood transfusions for wounded communist soldiers on several occasions.[24]

Since, Mrs. Pham did not speak English and the prisoner's only Vietnamese word was "soup,"[25] she could communicate with the American only when an English speaking PAVN soldier (again, proselytizing cadre) came to the hospital. Once while a PAVN was questioning the American she heard him say that his unit had withdrawn and left him after a firefight. She said the American gave her his address before he left the camp, but she misplaced it and could not recall it from memory.

As he recovered from his wounds the prisoner was given a book-like diary and he often wrote in it. When he left the hospital, he took the notebook with him in his backpack. She also recalled that he wrote a letter on at least one occasion and a 50-year-old officer from North Vietnam took the letter to censor it.

---

24 During her interviews, Mrs. Pham never called the American by name, but said on several occasions, she had heard other personnel refer to him as "Spot" or "Spart." This was the only American prisoner treated at the hospital during her tenure.

25 Don may have figured out that the soup was heated, killing organisms that would otherwise have made it difficult for him to keep it down.

Chapter 7

Mrs. Pham said Don was kind and very emotional. He was very fond of her and was very sad and cried if she had someone else care for him. However, if she went herself, he was happy and would eat a lot.

As Don's wounds healed, he made several attempts to escape. As a badly crippled patient, he was not closely guarded. He would not be able to travel far if he did escape, especially without food and water. Hospital personnel also knew local villagers would not help him for fear of retaliation by communist forces that controlled the area. Further, Don probably had little sense of where he was; especially in relation to where the nearest friendly forces might be found. Don was trapped by his condition and his circumstances. He knew his best hope for rescue was to be spotted by a helicopter and lifted out. Even that small hope was fraught with problems.

Generally, the wop-wop sound of twirling helicopter blades was a welcome sound, signaling arrival of supplies or a ride out of the jungle. For Don, however, sitting hour after hour hoping and praying for one of those helicopters to spot him, must have been excruciating. He had to worry, too, that in his blue pajamas, he might be mistaken for a NVA/VC and shot. It was a risk he was willing to take.

One night about 3 a.m., U.S. helicopters were active in the area. Now able to walk with a crutch, Don escaped from the hospital. Two days later he was carried back to the hospital by troops from the Tien Lanh Village Militia. Fortunately, he bore no signs of physical abuse and was not punished at the hospital for the escape attempt.

Another night he stole a set of white clothing and escaped to the top of a hill, apparently intending to signal passing aircraft. No aircraft came by during the two days he was gone. Hunger forced him to return to the hospital. Don tried to escape three times. One of those times, Assistant Pharmacist Mr. Thanh caught him and brought him back to the hospital.

Another time, when helicopters were hovering over the hospital, he fled for four days, but was returned when guards caught him drinking at a nearby stream. The guards were angry and intended to shoot him, but someone dissuaded them by explaining the prisoner of war policy. According to Mrs. Pham, Don appeared repentant from that time on and his conduct was perfect. She said he was very well liked, an impression supported by Mr. Nguyen Xuan Thanh, an Assistant Pharmacist at

CK-120. Mr. Thanh recalled that an American soldier matching Don's description was brought to the hospital with serious wounds to his right thigh and heel. An interpreter that accompanied the group told Mr. Thanh the soldier's name was "Don." At first the soldier could not eat rice like Vietnamese patients, so they cooked rice soup for him. The soldier was a very likeable person and everyone treated him as if he was any other patient.

After Don had been at CK120 for about eight months, the high command decided to send him to a rehabilitation center in anticipation of returning him to U.S. control. The hospital directed Mr. Trung, a guard, to escort the prisoner. Assistant Pharmacist Mr. Thanh and Mr. Khoi (a medic) were going in the same direction so they decided to travel together. Mrs. Phan Thi Phien, the Assistant Political Officer for CK120, also joined the group because she was meeting her husband so they could travel to their new duty station in North Vietnam.

At approximately 8:00 a.m. the group headed south along the Song Tranh. About three hours later they had lunch at the Cau Chim three-way intersection. Here, everyone bid farewell. Mrs. Phien met her husband and headed north. Mr. Thanh and Mr. Khoi went southeast along the Song Vang. Mr. Trung and Don continued west along the Song Tranh. This was the last time Mr. Thanh saw this U.S. soldier. When he returned about ten days later he heard that Mr. Trung had been killed in an ambush.

Witnesses were asked about the fate of Donald Sparks after he left the CK120 Hospital. None had first-hand knowledge; many offered hearsay that he was either shot while trying to escape or died of malaria in route to a POW camp in the mountains west of the Song Tranh. The Cau Chim three-way intersection is the last definitive location a reliable witness saw Don Sparks. The approximate date was February 1970.

MORE WHAT IFS

On September 18, 1969, thirteen months after the 3rd Platoon C Company, 5th/46th had assaulted into the vacated field hospital, a Civilian Irregular Defense Group from the Tien Phuoc Special Forces Camp captured two Vietnamese who said they could lead allied forces

Chapter 7

to two locations where they had seen an American (see sightings on Map 4). Two civilians confirmed the locations were in an area where civilians were not allowed, possibly to maintain security for a hospital or information about a POW. The location of these sightings was in the proximity of the vacated hospital the 3rd Platoon had confirmed a year earlier. Putting these two pieces of information together, the Intelligence Branch of the 196th Brigade and the Brigade Aviation Officer reportedly contemplated a recovery operation in conjunction with the Tien Phuoc Special Forces Detachment. The operation was never conducted.

Another event occurring during Don's time at CK 120 may have contributed to the decision not to attempt a rescue. On May 13, 1969, Larry Aiken was wounded and captured at the Battle for Nui Yon Hill. He was taken to Field Hospital CK130 located about 16 air miles southeast of CK 120. During a combat assault by American and ARVN forces in July, Larry was rescued. Unfortunately, the raid also resulted in additional wounding by his captors and on July 25 he died without regaining consciousness. After the location of CK130 was disclosed, the hospital was abandoned. Don was probably at or near CK 120 at the time of Larry's rescue from CK130. It is not known if the rescue had any effect on how Don was treated or where he was held.

We now know these two locations were likely part of or associated with CK-120 Hospital and the sightings were likely Don. Did the deadly outcome of the July 10, 1969 attempt to rescue Larry Aiken discourage taking another high-risk rescue endeavor? Did the rapid turnover of experienced American personnel contribute to the reluctance? We don't know.

It is impossible not to think "what if?" What if the rescue attempt for Larry had led to his successful recovery? What if the planned recovery operation had been carried out? What if any of these potential rescue opportunities hadn't been missed? Could Don have returned home and lived the life he had dreamed of?

CHAPTER 8

INTO THE MOUNTAINS

> Apparently, by February 1970, Don's value as a propaganda tool for communist forces had waned. He was no longer worth carrying in a hammock. Crippled and fevered, he was forced to limp wherever he was taken. The journey from the CK120 Hospital at Tien Lanh Village to the west side of the Song Tranh had to be excruciating.

AFTER LUNCH AT THE CAU CHIM CROSSROADS, Don was last seen going west by Assistant Pharmacist Mr. Nguyen Xuan Thanh. The end of his journey was to have been Jungle Camp, a prisoner of war camp northwest of Hanoi Mountain. Accounts by former POWs support the conclusion that Jungle Camp was Don's intended destination as he and his guard set off up the Song Tranh toward the Xa Steam drainage.

Major Floyd H. Kushner of the United States Army witnessed the death of Marine Lance Corporal Joseph Zantocki whose known burial site was confirmed as Jungle Camp. Major Kushner stated that a

VC interpreter had told him a U.S. Prisoner of War named "Don" was scheduled to join the group, but was unable to travel because of a foot wound. He was being held four to five days travel distance from Jungle Camp. Likewise, Marine SGT. Jose Jesus Anzadula, in an April 1973 debriefing, stated that NVA guards at Jungle Camp told him of Don's anticipated arrival. However, Don's transfer was not completed, a fact the NVA guard attributed to the soldier's foot wound.

As someone who liked people, Don would probably have looked forward to joining other American POWs, where he potentially would have companions with whom he could communicate. Obviously, this would still not be ideal, but it would be better than the isolation and loneliness he was likely experiencing at CK120. Tragically, as indicated above, he never arrived.

Where Don's trail ended along the travel route between Cau Chim Crossroads and Jungle Camp is unknown. There is evidence that on April 11 he was met by a proselytizing cadre at an unspecified location along the trail. What happened to Don beyond that point remains a mystery.

If Don's remains are to be found and returned to his family, they must be located somewhere in the vast area between Cau Chim Crossroads and Jungle Camp. At the time of Don's trek, the area was relatively unpopulated, dotted with small hamlets like the Thon bon Hamlets shown on Map 6. To narrow the search for Don's body, efforts were made to discover the route that he and his guard would most likely have followed. Even a hint of this information was a long time in coming.

Chapter 8

MAP 5
OVERVIEW OF LOCATIONS FROM THE SITE OF CAPTURE TO UNKNOWN LOCATION

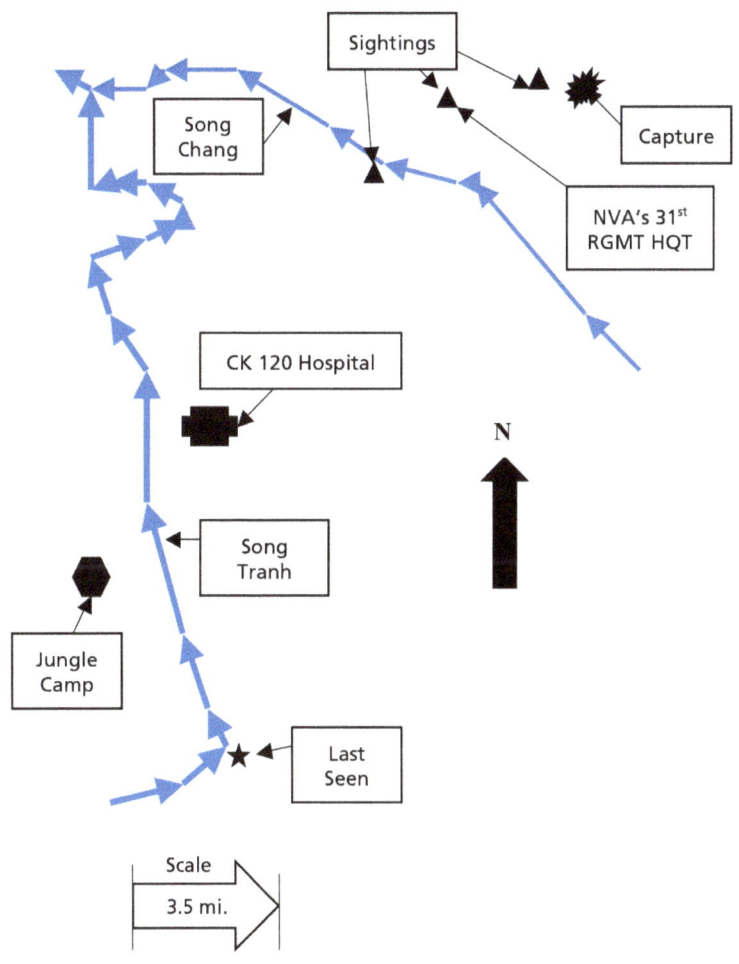

On June 17, 1969, Don Sparks was WIA and captured. Unable to walk, he was carried in a hammock. Three sighting locations suggest the approximate route used to transport him. He remained at a mobile hospital location for eight months. In February of 1970, using a make-shift crutch, he was led toward Jungle Camp, a mobile POW compound where other Americans were held. He never arrived. He was last seen at the Cau Chim Crossroads.

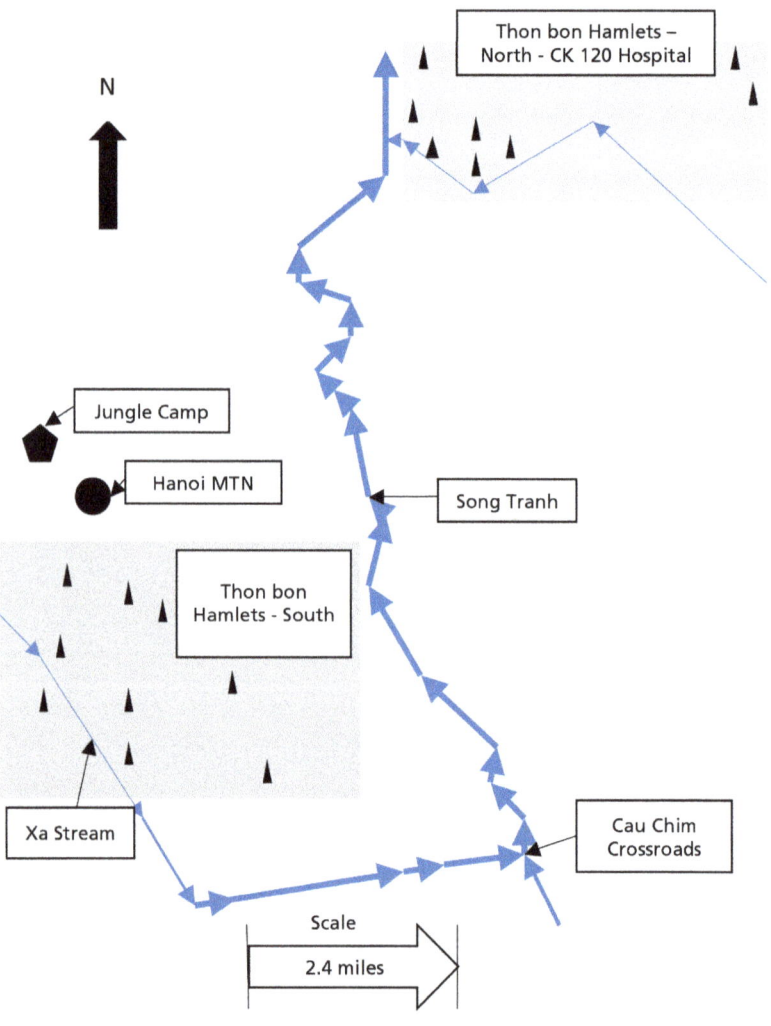

MAP 6
LOCATION OF TIEN LANH VILLAGE, THON BON HAMLETS, CAU CHIM CROSSROADS AND JUNGLE CAMP

In February 1970, Don Sparks was taken from CK 120 Hospital in Tien Lanh Village, Thon bon Hamlets - North, to the Cau Chim Crossroads. He was last seen moving west along the Song Tranh on the way to the Jungle Camp destination. The logical pathway would take him through Thon bon Hamlets- South. He never arrived.

Chapter 8

Almost thirty years after the fact, Mr. Doan Huu Nghi, the former political officer at CK120, was interviewed as part of a joint American/Vietnamese investigation. During that 1990 interview, Mr. Nghi was questioned along with Mrs. Hoang Thi Pham, who did most of the talking. At that time, Mr. Nghi did not indicate having knowledge of the route Don might have traveled.

Mr. Nghi was interviewed again in 2000 during a unilateral Vietnamese investigation. This time, at the age of 71 and very ill with kidney failure, he offered what remain the only clues to the travel route followed by Don and his guard. What accounts for his sharing this new information remains unclear. Perhaps he had learned more during the 10-year interval between interviews. Perhaps it was the skill of the interviewers or the accuracy of the recorders and translators. Perhaps the presence or absence of specific individuals allowed him to speak more freely. Perhaps Mr. Nghi's declining health induced a change of heart regarding the American POW. Whatever the cause, I and Don Sparks' family are grateful for the information he shared.

The general route described by Mr. Nghi went "up to Khe Hoa, over Ong Doc Mountain, up Xa Stream to Ca Camp in the Nguyen Chi Tranh area." Xa Stream leads to the south side of Hanoi Mountain. Map 6 illustrates the distance Don would have been challenged to traverse in his crippled and weakened condition.

The shared name and numbering of the Thon Bon hamlets suggests an historical connection among these geographically separated hamlets. The walk from Tien Lanh Village to the easiest to reach, low-elevation Thon bon – South Hamlets was on fairly gentle terrain. Still, a crippled, fevered prisoner hobbling with a crutch would be severely challenged. Traveling the easiest route between the two clusters of hamlets would have been logical, especially since economic, cultural, political, and familial relationships among all Thon bon Hamlets might provide support during this multi-day journey. Proceeding northward uphill from the Cau Chim Crossroads, Don and his guard would have encountered few inhabitants on the increasingly steep, less well-traveled trail.

Don's condition probably deteriorated as he coped with the rougher terrain. In addition, he was separated from medical personnel who might have treated his fever. Provisions on the trail were probably even less digestible than the rice soup he was eating at CK120. Finding clean drinking water to stay hydrated was probably a challenge. As night-time temperatures in the higher elevations dropped, shelter from the cold and rain may have been scarce. Considering these factors, it is difficult to estimate what distance Don and his guard could have covered in "four or five travel days." Further, we can only speculate what might have happened during that time. Did they stop somewhere hoping Don might recover if he had time to rest? Did they turn around and go back to a more inhabited area where help might be found? Did Don's guard leave him with someone in one of the Thon bon (South) Hamlets; or simply abandon him; or shoot him? The details of Don's final days remain shrouded in the past with the only certainty being he never arrived at Jungle Camp.

The area of Don's ordeal and death has changed a great deal since the end of the war in 1975. Satellite imagery shows that jungles have been cleared, even in fairly steep topography. Rivers have been dammed to form lakes. Roads have been built to replace trails. Developed communities have appeared where previously there were few if any permanent residents. Given these changes, landmarks that might be used to locate Don's remains are rapidly disappearing.

A potential burial site near Thon bon 13 was surveyed in August 1994 with no results. Local villagers had never heard of a burial site in the area—not surprising since the area was recently developed and most current inhabitants had arrived well after 1969. The survey site lay at the edge of road now entering an intensively developed housing area. Looking at this location on Google Earth underscores the urgency of searching for Don's remains. With each passing year, the likelihood of finding someone who remembers the whereabouts of an American soldier with a wounded heel and leg diminishes.

When Don's family learned the names of locations along the route from the Cau Chim Crossroads toward Jungle Camp, they submitted a request to Defense POW/MIA Accounting Agency (DPAA) on March 24, 2015 asking that an effort be made to determine the location of the place names. DPAA indicated they received the request, but communicated no additional information to Don's family, who followed up again on January 12, 2016. Again, DPAA indicated they received the request. At the time of this writing, no further communication has been received by the Sparks' family regarding the request. After a three-year silence, it is pretty safe to assume that DPAA is not going to respond. If the location of these places is known to DPAA, they have not been disclosed to the family.

During the rainy season, paper doesn't last long on the jungle floor. So these 2-sided NVA propaganda leaflets hadn't been there long. This shows their perspective of us and how the anti-war sentiment could be used against us. If the NVA proselytizing cadre could have extracted the words they wanted from Don, it might have been used in this type of psychological effort. It shows the limited extent of enemy familiarity with the English language. Proselytizing cadre and interpreters would likely be even less skilled than the leaflet author.

CHAPTER 9

LETTERS

LETTERS HOME

AS MENTIONED IN CHAPTER 7, DON WAS VISITED by proselytizing cadre during his time at CK120 hospital. The mission of the cadre officers was to elicit information that could be used either as negative propaganda against the U.S. or positive propaganda for the North Vietnamese. In addition to whatever interrogations he may have endured at CK120, Don was also visited by a proselytizing cadre on April 11, 1970 during his trip toward Jungle Camp.

As unpleasant as these visits must have been, they did afford Don an opportunity to write home. Because most of the cadre had marginal English skills, they probably couldn't understand much of what Don wrote. Being smart and having learned from previous "visits," Don probably tried to confirm that the two letters written on April 11 were actually written by him and that he was being held captive.

For purposes of readability, I have typed the text of the letters from scanned copies of the hand-written originals contained in case files

MAP 7
DONALD L. SPARKS IN VIETNAM
Proximity Map

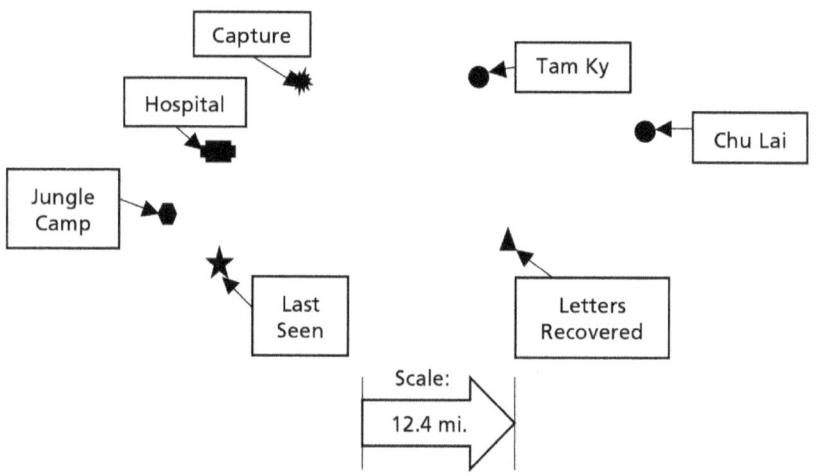

Don Sparks was captured 36 air miles west of the city of Tam Ky. He was carried in a hammock about 11 air miles to the southwest where he was held in a hospital for approximately eight months. He was last seen in February of 1970 at the Cau Chim Crossroads with a makeshift crutch, being led toward Jungle Camp. Letters he wrote April 11, 1970, were recovered May 17, 1970, about 23 miles east of his last seen location.

provided to Don's family by the Department of Defense, Defense POW/MIA Accounting Agency (DPAA). In transcribing the letters, I retained Don's grammar, punctuation, and spelling. The only detail I excluded was Don's American Express number, which in fact corresponded to his account and further substantiates that he wrote the letter.

Don wrote two letters, apparently one right after the other. When I looked closely at Don's handwriting in the first letter, it is normal cursive script. In the second letter, the handwriting initially looks normal, but further along the pressure applied on the left side of the page appears to be noticeably greater than on the right. I speculate that the proselytizing cadre were not satisfied with the content of the first letter and were holding Don in an awkward, painful position to extract comments that could be used as propaganda. Also, the change of tone in the second paragraph lends support to this impression. The criticism of U.S. policy, suggests he was being forced to add statements by the proselytizing cadre.

April 11, 1970

Everyone at Home:

I hope you have received the letters I have been writing. I have not heard or seen another American in nearly 10 months now, and I am longing for a letter from home. All this time I have continually been treated very well by the Vietnamese people. I can't thank them enough for their care.

I think of home all the time and surely hope you are all well and have been blessed with some happiness. I haven't forgotten your birthday Mom. I hope you took the day off, you truly deserve a rest. Then there is my kid brother. He is probably thinking of the service. He could probably get a hardship deferment and stay home if he wanted to. I don't want to run his life; I have trouble with my own. But I know I would have been encouraged to take over some responsibility if I had worked for a percent in a partnership with Dad. And talked about what crop or corn number to plant, the fertilizer program, whether it was a good time to sell livestock and beans, help keep records, and pay bills rather than just cash a check.

I have had a lot of time to think these past months. Often I am very ashamed of my past. All the times I was provided for and just took for granted. Good Mom and Dad were always there to take over when I neglected work, or got into trouble. I just hope to partially make up for it when I get home. Maybe you could see a recruiter about my income tax. I have an account (No.____) with the American Express and my pay vouchers should come home. If my records have been kept up to date. I should be an E-5 in relation to time and grade.

May God bless and keep you all.
Love,
Don

April 11, 1970

Dear DM:

I am very sorry there was a break in our correspondence. I truly hope you received the letter I wrote to you in October of last year.

My wounds have been healed for some time, but I am still very weak. Because of the wound to my foot, I will always have to use a crutch or stick to go about. So the journey to here was very painful to me. It will be well worth the pain I endured if it brings me closer to returning home. When I reach the U.S. I will definitely get a medical discharge from the Army, and I can go back to a civilian life. I have been in Vietnam for 11 months now with nearly 10 months of this time with the Vietnamese people. I carried a rifle for just a few days before I was wounded and did not fire it once. I am glad my conscience is clear of shooting another human being. All this time I have continually received good medical care, three meals each day, and treated in a very humane manner. I wish to thank your people for all the care I have been given.

In the United States I grew up on a farm and have studied agriculture. I understand many of the problems caused by the U.S. crimes and the hatred that has buill.[26] It may take years to establish a crop in the areas destroyed by bombs and chemical agents. These and many other hardships besides all the wounded and killed are created by this war. I hope peace will soon come to Vietnam and all Americans go home.

I understand the International Red Cross provides many services to POW's. If possible I would like to receive writing and reading materials here and hope they may contact my family (Mr + Mrs Calvin Sparks, RR#1 Carroll Iowa, Phone 712-659-3054) So my parents can write to me at my present address.

I want to thank you for any help you can give me, and I will try to continue writing to you.

Sincerely,
Donald L. Sparks

The greeting of DM in the second letter is an acronym Don often used for Dad and Mom in letters written before his capture. This was probably another purposeful clue Don used to signal his parents that he was actually writing the letter. Unfortunately, the U.S. government personnel who took possession of the letters when they were discovered did not understand to whom the second letter was addressed. They thought Don might have been writing to some unknown entity. Thus, the government officials spent months puzzling over the matter before (under pressure) releasing it to his parents, the intended recipients.

---

26 This is not a typo in the transcription but a mistake in the original. It suggests the Proselytizing Cadre had Don in pain and the last thing he was thinking of was crossing the "t." This is supported by content of the two sentences that follow.

These two letters are the only direct communication we have from Don after his capture. While they contain a grim indication of his plight, condition, and circumstances, they also tell us he had not given up hope of returning home. His Christian faith (Presbyterian) is reflected in his concern for others, not only his family, but also his captors. There was no vengeance in his heart. He was glad his conscience was clear of shooting another human being. This is after ten months of deprivation we can hardly fathom. Family and friends are blessed to have known Don Sparks.

OFFICIAL CORRESPONDENCE

Don Sparks' Date of Expected Return from Overseas (DEROS) was May 12, 1970, one month after he wrote the above two letters. Assuming he was still alive and aware of the date, it must have been especially painful to know he would not be rejoining family and friends as scheduled. Ironically, on May 12, an unknown author wrote two letters advocating a change in Don's status from MIA to KIA, body not recovered.

What caused the issue of Don's status to re-emerge at just this time is unknown. Perhaps his DEROS status triggered something in his file. Or it may have been that General Lloyd Ramsey (who had rejected the Board of Inquiry's recommendation of KIA status for Don) was returning to the States. Because almost all soldiers had a one-year tour of duty, anyone who could legitimately claim to have witnessed the ambush of June 17 would soon return home. So, designating Don's status as KIA would have brought closure to his file and required no further effort on his behalf or that of his family. This would have been a convenient resolution for the Army.

As stated in Chapter 1, I contacted Don's remaining family in 2014. Disappointed by the lack of information they had from the men who were there and a sense of loyalty to my long-ago friend, I undertook a search for Don's ultimate fate. The information in the remainder of this chapter paints a picture fraught with miscommunication, no communication and indifference for the suffering of Don's family. I begin my account with the following letter whose author asserts that Don was killed during the ambush.

~

DEPARTMENT OF THE ARMY
Company C, 3d Battalion, 21st Infantry
196th Infantry Brigade, Americal Division
APO San Francisco 96374
AVDF-BBBB-CCO

Subject: Statement

Commanding General
Americal Division
ATTN: AVDF-AGRM
APO San Francisco 96374

1. In reviewing the facts of the case concerning the status of PFC Donald L. Sparks, Co C 3d Bn 21st Inf, 196th Inf Bde, I feel that there have been some very important facts left out. I was present on 17 June 1969 when the first platoon of Co C, 3d Bn 21st Inf walked into an NVA ambush of an undetermined size. PFC Sparks was the second man of the point squad. I wasn't close enough to him to see if he were wounded or not, but the men who were, definitely stated that he was hit at very close range with small arms fire, and machine gun fire.

2. Because of the heavy enemy fire, first platoon was forced to pull back leaving the bodies of PFC Sparks and PFC Graham behind, affirmed that both men were indeed dead. An air strike was called on that location, and then second platoon of Co C, 3d Bn 21st Inf attempted to move in to recover the bodies. Their point man got within visual sight of both bodies when he came under heavy fire, forcing

second platoon to pull back. He confirmed that both bodies were stripped of all military clothing and gear except their boots.

3. Later that same day, more air strikes were called with 500 lb bombs, and 1000 lb bombs with delayed fuses. What was once a thickly vegetated hill was reduced to barren rubble. The third platoon of Co C, 3d Bn 21st Inf returned to this location on the morning of 18 June 1969. They recovered the body of PFC Graham, but couldn't locate any remains of PFC Sparks. Where his body was stated to be by the eyewitnesses, was a huge crater, obviously created by one of the 1000 lb. bombs. It was at least 8 feet deep, and about 20 feet in diameter. We spent that whole day and most of the next day digging up ground in that whole region in hopes of recovering PFC Sparks' body, but with negative results. We did discover what appeared to be a makeshift NVA grave, with parts of a body buried there. The parts were so decimated, that it was impossible to tell if they were remains of PFC Sparks, or of one of the NVA soldier's.

4. It is my opinion that PFC Sparks' remains were totally destroyed by the air strikes, and hence his body was never recovered.

August J. Weidner
SP4, Co C 3d Bn 21st inf

It is not clear what prompted the author to write this letter or what qualified him to assert the facts he laid out. A number of his "facts" are inconsistent with information I gathered from telephone interviews with those having first-hand knowledge of the ambush. In addition, to

Chapter 9

the above letter, a second one, signed by Dean G. Christy, also contained misinformation. The following chart highlights these inconsistencies.[27]

Assertions in Letters	Information Calling Assertions into Question
"Their point man got within visual sight of both bodies when he came under heavy fire, forcing 2nd Platoon to pull back. He confirmed that both bodies were stripped of all military clothing and gear except their boots."	The point man for the 2nd Platoon received a gunshot wound to the head and died instantly. He would not have been able to confirm anything about the ambush. A single boot with Don's dog tag in the boot lace was found at the scene.
The destruction caused by the bombing indicated that napalm was also dropped on the site.	Squad leader Joel Pasternack indicated no napalm had been used and that 250 lb. fragmentation bombs, not 500 or 1000 lb. bombs, were most likely used in the single airstrike.
Don's body was completely destroyed or buried in the airstrike, or the enemy carried it off thinking it was one of their own.	One month earlier (May 1969) Company C recovered five bodies from a previous incident after an airstrike that included the use of napalm. In that incident, the one body not recovered had not been killed, but had been captured.[28] The remaining bodies were all recovered and identified suggesting that the company's leadership in June 1969 had abundant experience with recovery of bodies and understood how unlikely it was that the body was completely destroyed.
We did discover what appeared to be a makeshift NVA grave, with parts of a body buried there. The parts were so decimated, that it was impossible to tell if they were remains of PFC Sparks, or of one of the NVA soldier's.	Don was 5ft. 11in., weighted 165 pounds, had blue eyes, and brown hair. That is hardly the description of a typical Vietnamese

---

27 A careful reading of both letters suggested to me they were written—but not signed—by one individual. I have made no further effort to identify the actual author, as by now it is not relevant. I do, however, want to offer a cautionary note to any family that might, in the future, deal with a MIA/POW situation. It is important to know that, for whatever reason, an attempt could be made to make the case go away.
28 Larry Aiken was the soldier captured in the May 13, 1969 Battle for Nui Yon Hill.

As I reflect on the above discrepancies, I feel an undeniable anger. The Board of Inquiry's original recommendation did not change the reality of Don's MIA status. To me, it appears someone was intent on adding information to his file that would change Don's status to KIA, body not recovered. Knowing that Don was alive on April 11, 1970 and very possibly alive on May 12, 1970, it is hard to accept that any fellow soldier would want to close the case on him. To help temper my anger, I remind myself of the following.

1. The belief that Don was dead was based on statements gathered by the Board of Inquiry that unequivocally state Don was dead. Those statements can be categorized as faulty, incorrect, or false, depending on one's point of view. I chose to describe them as "incorrect." The statements are not signed, but initialed.

2. August J. Weidner and Dean G. Christy had infantry status, but were working as C Company clerks in the rear. In a 2015 phone interview, I read to August Weidner the document he had signed in 1970. Much to his credit, he was very honest and forthright with me. He recalled that he had been in the field with 3rd Platoon on June 17, 1969 and had a vague memory of searching for someone. However, he had no specific knowledge of the incident in question. Furthermore, he was certain that he had never done anything like dig up a nearby grave or find body parts that couldn't be confirmed as NVA or American. "That is clearly something I would not forget," August stated. I learned from August that Dean Christy had died but the circumstances for signing the documents were the same. Namely, when you are an infantryman working in the rear, you sign what you are told to or risk being sent back to the field. Signing documents with their names or someone else's name was routine. At the time, the letter was just another document.

3. Jim Gordon was C Company Commander from August 1969 to December 1969. Dennis O'Neill succeeded him from December 1969 to May 1970. In a 2017 phone interview, Dennis confirmed that prior to his appointment as company commander, he had been the 3rd Platoon Leader. However, he was not yet in the field on June 17, 1969. He was unaware of Don's capture including any of the documentation surrounding it. Dennis thought highly of both August Weidner and Dean Christy who had served as his Radio Telephone Operator in the 3rd Platoon. This confirmed my own positive assessment of August Weidner. Dennis supported August's statement that Dean also had infantry status and could be sent back to the field at any time he displeased the leadership. When I told Dennis that Dean had passed away, he was moved by the news. He commented that Dean was a very humane person who did not belong out there (in the field), but had always done his job in every way.[29]

4. I do not believe the author of these letters had any intent to harm Don or his family. The rationalization that "he must be dead" prevailed. At the time, I don't believe they visualized those statements being available to Don's family.

5. The letters did not materially influence the categorization of Don's status. In the June 1970 annual review of his case, the receipt of the letters was acknowledged as additional information not provided by the Board of Inquiry statements. However, it also stated "the validity of their conclusions is questionable."

Five days after August and Dean signed "their" letters, an unexpected event would debunk the tale of "his body was destroyed

---

29 Both Jim Gordon and Dennis O'Neill were very professional and helpful as I tried to find out what happened to Don Sparks. I greatly appreciate their assistance and their obvious respect for the men who sacrificed so much.

by the bombing or the enemy mistakenly thought his body was that of a Vietnamese."

Don would never know his April 11 letters would find their way into American hands or ever make it home as he had hoped. Presumably, the letters passed from the proselytizing cadre to a political officer who carried them 30 miles east to Dragon Valley, near Hill 371 on the north side of the Quan River. At approximately 3:40 pm on May 17, 1970, someone from 1st Platoon, C Company, 5th BN 46th BDE, Americal Division, killed the political officer and recovered Don's letters. Short, propaganda-type notes were scribbled on the letters in Vietnamese, suggesting there never was an intention to mail them. In all likelihood, the letters were being transported to be interpreted and potentially used to promote the communist cause by embarrassing the United States.

My efforts to learn more about this incident from someone from 1st Platoon have failed. First Lieutenant Gary Mower, 1st Platoon Leader that day, would have been likely to remember the recovery of two GI letters. Unfortunately, at 6:55 PM on May 21, while preparing the company's night defensive perimeter, a booby-trapped 81 mm mortar round blew off both of his legs. Lieutenant Mower made it through the surgery, but died the next day. Captain Smith, the Company Commander would also likely have knowledge of the event; but has not been located since his departure from Vietnam.

CORRESPONDENCE WITH THE "THE WORLD"

On April 19, 1970, the Sioux City Iowa Journal published a letter critical of the Vietnam War from SP 4 Dave Krommenhoek. In response, Mrs. Ernest Kaufmann sent Dave a letter. He in turn responded. Following are excerpts from his May 17, 1970 letter.

> I am a radio operator in the tactical operations center. We are in direct communication with the guys out in the field so I know most of what goes on in my battalion. I work where the companies get birds for resupply, mail, ammo and weapons. They also get all their artillery support plus air support such as gunships, bombers, fighters and

reconnaissance planes. We also supply them with dust offs or medevac helicopters. You don't know what a heart break it is to call a dust off for a man who has stepped on a mine and had both legs torn off.

An incident today concerns a letter taken off a dead VC. It was written by a man who was captured. The letter was dated April 11th. This man has been in Nam 12 months and a prisoner for 11 months. He was wounded and has received medical aid but it must have been very poor medical aid because with the minor wound he described he should be able to walk with no problem. In his letter he said he uses a stick for a crutch. In 11 months he received nothing from home and has no idea what has happened at home. And by the way he is from Carroll, Iowa."

To follow this lead about Don's fate, I contacted Dave by telephone and email in 2016. From this I learned that his Tactical Operations Center S-2 was housed on one end of a building and an office of Intelligence (S-3) at the other end. The documents recovered from the political officer KIA by 1st Platoon C Co were delivered to the Intelligence office. Because Dave was from Iowa, Intelligence asked him to read the letters and confirm that the zip code did indeed indicate an Iowa address. Dave verified that Carroll was a town in Iowa.

When Mrs. Kaufmann received Dave's letter, she contacted the Sioux City Journal to seek assistance in determining who the man from Carroll might be. On June 5, 1970, she wrote to the Mayor of Carroll, Iowa who, in turn, forwarded her letter to Calvin Sparks. From Mrs. Kaufman, Calvin also obtained SP4 David Krommenhoek's address and sent him a letter on June 12, 1970.

Less than a week after hearing about Don's letters, the Sparks family coincidentally received a letter from LT. Col. William N. Batt, Jr., the Survivor Assistance Officer assigned to their family. One of Batt's duties was to send a letter of condolence to the family on the anniversary of Don's becoming MIA. In response, Calvin contacted Lt. Col. Batt and requested his help in recovering Don's letters.

Don's letters, complete with his parents name, address, and phone number, had been given to the Joint Personnel Recovery Center on May 22, 1970, a month before Calvin and Arloha learned of their existence. Apparently, no one from the United States Army had the authority, time, inclination, or decency to pick up the phone and tell Don's parents what had been found. Instead, the news trickled to them through unofficial channels from a radio operator to a private citizen who cared enough to follow-up and get word to Don's family. Another "what if?" Had this informal channel of communication not worked, would the family ever have been told about the recovered letters?

David Krommenhoek's superiors were not pleased with his letters. One in particular wanted to court martial him. The Sparks' family spoke in his defense, and the Army decided not to pursue the action. I suspect the potential for publicity and exposure of their own communication incompetence might have helped them reach that conclusion.[30]

On August 10, 1970, Don's letter to "Everyone at Home" reached his family. Because David Krommenhoek had mentioned information in the second letter (e.g., use of crutch or stick to walk), Calvin and Arloha suspected they had not been given everything the Army had recovered. They pursued the missing letter through Colonel Batt and in January of 1971, finally received a copy of the letter addressed to "DM." The family could then clarify the conundrum of DM's identity (Dad and Mom) —a puzzle that could have been solved months earlier had the Intelligence office or the Personnel Recovery Center simply contacted the Sparks family when the letters first came to light.[31] Again, no communication.

For Calvin and Arloha Sparks, I can hardly imagine the mixed feelings. On the one hand, elated to know that as recently as April 11, 1970, their son was alive and had written letters. What a welcome burst of hope that he would return home. On the other hand, their confidence in the United States Army and the government it represented had nose

---

30 When I spoke with David, I thanked him for what he had done and expressed my concern that the Sparks family would never have learned of their son's letters were it not for his actions. Dave explained that his release of the information was less intentional than the one superior thought. He then added he had no regrets.

31 Again, who was at fault doesn't matter. The point is for any future POW family to be aware of this pathetic failure of communication.

dived. If they ever had trusted Westmoreland's promise,[32] it was now exposed as hollow bureaucratic lip-service.

The family did not receive a copy of the withheld letter until January of 1971 because it was purportedly "classified." It was released to them shortly before declassification. If only the Army would have trusted the family enough to ask. Don probably used DM as an additional means of letting his family know that, yes, it was really him. What he didn't count on was U.S. Army's distrust of those who had the most to gain, his family. While people like Colonel William Batt had worked hard to help the family and had earned their trust, there were people on the other end of the trust spectrum undermining all that he accomplished.

At the time of this writing, the family still has not been given the original letters or even had the opportunity to see them. Dave Krommenhoek is the only person other than official case investigation personnel known to have seen them. Presumably, they are still in a case folder, somewhere.

The Department of Defense had the hand writing in the recovered letters compared to hand writing on Don's last letters sent home before his capture. Calvin and Arloha sent copies of his June 10 and 16, 1969 letters. Their analysis confirmed the hand writing was that of Donald Lee Sparks.

---

32 *"As soon as any additional information is received, the Adjutant General will pass it on to you without delay."* Letter from General William Westmoreland dated July 6, 1969.

CHAPTER 10

RE-ENTERING THE WORLD

> Given what Don was coping with in the early months of 1970, my adjustment back in *The World* seems mild. Still the abrupt transition from life in the jungle to home required some getting used to. I recount my re-entry with a sense of sadness that Don never had a chance for re-entering *The World*.

LOOKING OUT OF THE WINDOW OF THE FREEDOM BIRD that flew me out of Vietnam, I recognized the snow-covered summit of Mt. Fuji. I wasn't going home yet, but for now, I was happy to settle for the 249th Evac Hospital at Camp Drake outside of Tokyo, Japan.

On the second day in Japan, what had happened started to sink in more deeply. I was moving beyond just being glad to be alive and starting to think about my wound. The doctors and nurses had been telling me, "Don't worry, we can fix that. It is going to take a while, but it will get better." I remember at one point going into a stall in the bathroom, closing the door, and crying—convinced I was going to be a cripple, a gimp. Those are terrible words to use, but they dominated my negative thoughts. Finally, I thought of the people in the ward whose wounds made mine look like a cat scratch. I pulled myself together and never acted like that again.

I wanted to get out of that hospital and away from the Army. I was pretty certain I was near Tokyo so there would be things to do, but the Army was not about to let me out of its sight. I was stuck in the hospital for a week, before departing on an Air Force hospital plane to Travis Air Force Base in California. A fellow passenger was barely hanging on to life; staff onboard were prepared to deal with his crisis. Again, how fortunate I was. When the wheels of the plane touched down in California, it felt wonderful to be back in the good old USA. I had been gone less than six months, but it was the longest six months of my life. I later realized the passage of time was normal for many at home; for me, it had slowed to a crawl.

In the hospital ward at Travis a black soldier was sitting on his bed, not moving or saying anything. A somewhat slightly older white patient said to him, "don't worry about making your bunk, I will help you." Suddenly, it registered, "My God, he's blind. That's why he's so still." I should have reached out, too. Not knowing what to say, I said nothing.

Two USO "donut dollies"[33] said I could make a free phone call home. Yes! I wanted to let my family know I was safely back in the United States. In a private room, one volunteer offered to dial the number for me. While dialing, she started to cry and couldn't stop. I was okay, but she was overwhelmed. Dad answered the phone; Mom wasn't home. I didn't say much other than I was back and doing okay.

My next flight took me to Denver, Colorado, and Fitzsimmons Army Hospital in the nearby suburb of Aurora. In route, I noticed a handsome, athletic-looking 19 or 20-year old soldier whose lower arm was amputated. Since I had a gunshot wound to my left arm, I was keyed on anyone missing an arm; mindful I could have been in the same circumstance. He had that "most popular in the class" look, but

---

33 This was an old WWII term used to describe the young women volunteers with the USO. While many of their peers were protesting the Vietnam War, these two young women chose to be supportive of soldiers returning under different circumstances than expected. I thanked them profusely, and God bless them.

Chapter 10

without the accompanying arrogance. I pictured him in high school as the envy of all the guys and the dream of all the girls. On our arrival, his parents and girlfriend were among the families meeting the wounded. Since no one was meeting me, I was free to absorb the occasion without distraction. It was a stirring moment, but one lacking the privacy it deserved. I sensed his greeters had tried to prepare themselves mentally, but there was still the shock of that first-time visual. Like me, they probably thought, "It could have been much worse." For many, it was. And like so many others, this family was facing the reality that life would never be what it would have been before the War intervened.

My previous stateside experience in the Army was as a low-ranking trainee. Only rarely was I treated with compassion or respect. Patients wore blue pajamas that did not show rank. I was shocked in the chow line at Fitzsimmons when a server looked at me and said, "You look like you could use an extra one of these," and then placed a second pork chop on my plate. I left the States as a PFC and returned as a PFC, but here at the hospital I had apparently gained status. That kindness is still remembered with gratitude.

Christmas was rapidly approaching, and the Army was trying to get every recent, able-bodied Vietnam returnee home. I don't know if special accommodations were made, but amazingly, I was able to get a flight to Des Moines. While many service men in uniform were not being treated well in airports across the nation, I did not encounter any unpleasant confrontations.

On the way home from the airport, Mom explained that our dog, Sheppy, wouldn't be there. Several weeks earlier he had been hit by a car and killed. She hadn't told me in a letter because she was concerned that it might unnecessarily upset me. While I loved the dog, I was accustomed to handling bad news and would have been fine. She also told me that our across-the-road neighbor and Mom's really good friend Myra had recently passed away. With the recent bad news out of the way, we could concentrate on the good.

I commented that obviously, I had no Christmas gifts for them. My mother replied that having me home was the best gift they could ever have. We agreed we wouldn't chase after anything material and just focus on being together.

On December 23, 1969, I was so happy to be home on our farm. Just two weeks earlier, I had been firing a machine gun in Vietnam. Now, I was sitting in my father's chair with my arm in a gismo that held my fingers up with rubber bands. Looking out the window at our farmstead, I thought about all that had happened. When I left Iowa in June, I weighed 185 pounds; now I was 165. Although I didn't know it at the time, Don Sparks would never have that "I made it, I'm so happy to be home" moment.

The Sunday after Christmas, wearing my uniform, I went to Pleasant Hill Methodist Church with my parents. I had already seen our close neighbors, the Warrick's and Carl Elrod, but seeing everyone from church was another special moment. To them it probably seemed like I had been gone a few short months, but for me, it had been a very long time.

In a few days, I became sick with malaria and spent a week in the Veterans Hospital in Des Moines. I was tickled that Bill and Karen Elrod led several friends from my high school graduating class to the hospital for a visit. It was a wonderful welcome home.

On February 10, 1970, I had surgery on my arm to set the stage for recovery. It went well, and I was soon given another leave to return home. Exercise was a prescribed therapy, so I did appropriate work on the farm. There was always work on the farm, even in winter, even with a recovering functional arm.

I could drive so I went to Iowa State University. As I walked down a familiar corridor in Bessey Hall, I spotted Dr. Thomson, my academic advisor and mentor, emerge from a room down the hall. As he glanced my way, he stopped suddenly. His first words were "Well, I see they got you." I don't remember what I said, but it should have been "yes, but at least I am here."

I saw a few of my undergraduate friends. When I told good friends Rosemary Sailor and Ellen Hellman about being wounded, I almost cried. They didn't know what to say. I didn't blame them; how could they relate to that? We never talked about the rightness or wrongness of the war. I don't know how they felt about it. At that time, it was the elephant in the room for many people. A short silence was followed by a change of subject.

I found Norm and Dorene Kammin. Norm had also lived in Dodds House, and I had introduced him to Dorene. As Norm said in a

Christmas card 48 years later, "I still remember the relief we felt when you showed up at our door in Ames—wounded, but alive."

I called Barb, the friend who had given me an indifferent send off in San Francisco, and told her I was home early because I had been wounded. We set a time to meet at her apartment in Ames, but when I arrived, I found a note on the door. "I've gone down town to meet some friends. If you are in town again, give me a call." I just stood there, staring at it for a while. I paced around a little. This wasn't quite the welcome home I was hoping to receive. Obviously, she had no interest in me, and I needed to move on. It hurt, even though she certainly had never given me any indication she was serious about me. I had written twice when I was in Vietnam. She never answered. Hint! Hint! I left the note on the door untouched, walked away and never tried to contact her again. A more mature, less desperate 24-year-old college graduate would have figured it out sooner. I was too embarrassed to mention this to anyone. Sometimes when fellow Vietnam veterans say "welcome home,"[34] this memory comes back. Now, I chuckle about my over sensitivity. But then, the loneliness wasn't at all funny.

I flew standby from Des Moines to Cincinnati to see my good friends Craig and Becky Petre. The flight crew was so respectful they put me in first class and brought me all the free scotch and soda I wanted. It was a good thing the flight wasn't long. By the time I deplaned, I was buzzed. I don't know if Craig and Becky noticed, but I am sure I gave Becky an extra big hug and Craig a very warm hand shake.

Soon I was back at Fitzsimmons sharing time with fellow former grunts. Protests of the war were common, but we seldom mentioned it. After I returned home, the My Lai massacre by a Company in the Americal Division had become public knowledge, and the resulting public outrage was in the national news. Typical of me, I offered no opinion and didn't really want to hear one. I kept thinking, however, "What the hell was going on? My God, we never did anything like that. Did that really happen?" Yes, it had, but I was not inclined to discuss it.

About March of 1970, I was walking down a hospital hallway and saw a fellow patient in standard-issue, blue pajamas coming toward me on crutches. He was missing one of his lower legs. As we passed, I

---

[34] "Welcome home" became a greeting among fellow veterans sometime after the war ended.

recognized him as my former company commander who had welcomed me to the bush eight months earlier. I stopped, turned around, and said "Captain Pate." (Was I supposed to say Sir?) He stopped, turned, and looked at me with no recognition, but "Yes."

"I was in Delta, first of the 8th," I reminded him.

"Oh, are you doing OK?" was his reply.

"Yes, I just got shot in the arm."

"Well, OK, take care," he said and turned and maneuvered down the hall. He was certainly more damaged than I, but looking around that hospital, we both had to know we got out in better condition than many.

In late April, 1970, I was granted a month of leave from Fitzsimmons Army Hospital with the understanding that I would go home to Iowa and stay therapeutically active. With spring field work on the way, that would be easy. On the evening of April 30, 1970, President Richard Nixon appeared on TV and announced a military crossing into Cambodia to deny the enemy access to known sanctuaries. I was immediately alert when I heard the 1st Air Cavalry would be one of the Divisions to cross the border at locations known as the Parrot's Beak and the Fishhook. The news fostered a strange, contradictory feeling. In one sense, I was glad to be home. On the other hand, I felt like I should be with my squad, as they were likely to be part of the operation.

May 1, 1970, the perceived expansion of the war (temporary or not) into Cambodia intensified public outrage. Protests against the Cambodian Invasion (Incursion) were especially prevalent on university campuses. On Monday, May 4, Vietnamese forces killed 24 young GIs. On the same date, the Ohio National Guardsmen killed four and wounded nine Kent State students. People were shocked. The 24 young casualties in Vietnam garnered no particular attention because that number was not much different than the 22 who died the day before or the 48 who perished the day after. Casualties of war were expected; casualties on campus were not.

Veishea, Iowa State's spring celebration, was scheduled for the weekend following the Kent State shooting. Protests were occurring that week on the Iowa State Campus and in the surrounding city of Ames. I was oblivious. That type of activism didn't happen at the Iowa State University I knew. More familiar was "Moo-U," a mocking, semi-derogatory name referring to the school's agricultural tradition where students were academically serious, politically conservative, and uninvolved with world affairs.

I drove from Prairie City to the campus on Saturday, May 9, 1970, the day of the Veisha parade. I went with no plans to meet anyone in particular, but seeking peer companionship and a sense of reconnection. My left arm was still in the contraption supporting my wrist and fingers. Combined with my military-style-short haircut, I stuck out like a sore thumb. I watched the parade and the "March of Concern" that followed. While I was standing between Beardshear Hall and the Memorial Union, a float went by with music playing Henry Mancini's "The Sweetheart Tree." I loved that song, and still do. It is a marker of the time.

The 5,000 protesters that followed were peaceful and orderly. I was struck by the number of people I recognized, but didn't know by name. Obviously, they were against the war. I took their disapproval personally, interpreting it as a condemnation of me and my former squad mates who, I correctly assumed, were in Cambodia. I don't remember talking to anyone; I was in a crowd, but felt alone. I didn't know where I belonged, but this wasn't it. My student days were over. I'd had enough. I went to my car and left for home.

While in Vietnam I had written to a girl I dated during the 1967-Summer of Love. She was gracious enough to write back even though she had moved on with her life. Driving home from Iowa State, I remembered she had written that The Vietnam War was something you had to decide which side you were on and stick with it. Generally, that is what most people did; including me. I was on the side of the guys who watched my back while I watched theirs. The guys who pulled my guard duty when I was so sick I was up and down all night. And yes, the guys who continued fighting when I was wounded and helped me survive.

CHAPTER 11

ANGUISH

"Extensive and continuous aerial and ground searches are being conducted and leaflets have been dropped announcing the offer of rewards for the recovery of missing personnel. As soon as any additional information is received, the Adjutant General will pass it on to you without delay."

LETTER FROM GENERAL WILLIAM C. WESTMORELAND'S OFFICE
JULY 5, 1969

JULY 6, 2017. ESTA AND I ARE DRIVING DOWN the rural Carroll County roads where her brother Don had traveled many times in his pre-Vietnam years. These gravel-surfaced roads have a familiar feel, like the roads in my home county. These dusty, backcountry, Iowa roads haven't changed much in the forty-eight years and three weeks since a shiny U.S. Army sedan carrying two, spit-polished officers traveled them. Esta remembers that day as though no time has passed.

She and brother Russell were helping their father, Calvin, sort hogs when the sedan pulled into the driveway. Calvin told them to finish; then walked the short distance to the house and joined Arloha in the front yard. Later, Calvin said it was like watching himself in a movie, except this was no movie; it was real life.

The officers probably followed protocol, identified themselves and confirmed they were speaking to the parents of Donald Lee Sparks. Since they were in a rural setting with no audience of neighbors, they dispensed with the suggestion to go inside the house. Then they uttered the words no parent wanted to hear. "The Secretary of the Army regrets to inform you that your son, PFC Donald Lee Sparks, is missing in action in Vietnam." The officers left, having nothing else to say.

Esta and Russell finished with the hogs and joined their parents in the grief-stricken moment. Calvin and Arloha went into the classic old farmhouse for a few moments of solitude before coming back out to face their world forever changed—for Don, for them, and for their remaining children Esta, Russell and Ron.

On that long-ago day, they faced the anguish of not knowing if Don was alive or dead. Was he wounded, in pain, scared, cold, hot, hungry and alone? Was he being tortured? What should they do next? How could they help their son? What thoughts raced in their minds; what ache lodged in their hearts?

As Esta described that day, my mind darted back to the 1979 movie *Friendly Fire* starring Carol Burnett and Ned Beatty, which depicts a scene in which a sedan pulls into their driveway and they immediately know the significance of the car's arrival. "Was it like that for you?" I asked. Although Esta had not seen *Friendly Fire,* she had watched a similar movie scene and confirmed that was basically the same experience. As we drove the country roads and talked, never far from my thoughts was the reality, "That could have been you, Arlyn. What happened to Don's parents 48 years ago could have happened to mine."

When we arrived at the Sparks' farmstead, we found a young man working near our parking spot. Esta introduced me as Don's college roommate to Don's nephew, one of many nieces and nephews Don never had a chance to meet. As I looked around, I noticed old buildings that were certainly present when Don lived there with his parents and siblings. I excused myself to take some photos, but Esta soon joined me. We talked about how things had been 48 years ago. We flipped

Chapter 11

an old derelict switch once used to pump water for the livestock. She pointed to a tool shed Ron and Don had re-organized as part of a 4-H project. When Don's brother Russell returned home, he showed us a picture of the farmstead as it appeared in 1908 when people farmed with horses. There was a rich history to the farmstead long before the Sparks family moved into its modest house. Don was supposed to have been a continuation of that history.

I could easily picture Don here. During our time at Iowa State, we talked about farm life. Don loved this way of life and the community he was a part of. In those innocent college days, I never dreamed anything so devastating would happen to him. Of all the fellow veterans and fellow grunts I have known, it is still hard to believe this happened to Don.

Following notification that Don was MIA, LTC William Batt was assigned to the Sparks family as their Survival Assistance Officer.[35] LTC Batt served as their contact with the Department of Defense, Secretary of the Army and they remember him warmly as someone who did all he could to help during that tumultuous time.

Calvin was the family's spokesperson, maintaining communication with the government to find out, "What do we do?" In addition, Calvin responded to the press and to family friends and community who offered their support. The family decided to remain positive that Don was still alive and hopeful that he would return home.

Calvin and Arloha received a letter dated August 8, 1969 from the Major General of the Army with more details of what purportedly happened to Don on June 17, 1969. It references a Board of Inquiry (BOI) made by officers. This is undoubtedly the June 26, 1969 BOI at LZ Center.

Following is an excerpt from that letter:

> Donald and another individual were in the front of the platoon when they were attacked and both were wounded by automatic weapons fire. Witnesses to the incident stated that Donald had received wounds to the head and stomach area, however, none of the witnesses were able to physically exam him for signs of life. One of the witnesses stated that

---
35 Also referred to as a Family Service Assistance Officer.

he had seen two North Vietnamese troops standing near your son and that he had been striped of his rifle, helmet, and other military equipment.

The three statements indicating that Don was definitely believed to be dead were excluded from the letter. The immediate anguish the above words had to cause his parents is hard to comprehend. It leaves the impression the witnesses must have thought Don was alive. Were the witness's American soldiers? It doesn't say. If the witness who saw the two NVA was an American soldier, and Don was on the ground, but the witness was close enough to see Don's wounds, couldn't the witness fire at the NVA? These questions could have rolled over and over in their minds, night after sleepless night.

As discussed in Chapter 9, "Letters," I believe the above excerpt was misinformation. I called it incorrect. At this point, determining who was responsible for the misinformation isn't relevant. While I am certain it caused considerable anguish, the relevant thing is the family decided to lay the anguish aside and move forward with the positive belief that Don was alive.

In May of 1970, their belief was substantiated when the Sheriff of Carroll County informed Calvin that a letter signed by Don had been recovered (see "Letters"). While this information did not come through the official channels he had expected, Calvin and the entire Sparks family were encouraged by the wonderfully hopeful news. Their decision to maintain a positive belief that Don was alive was correct. It didn't bring Don home, but at least they had the mental comfort of knowing they had not given up while Don was still alive.

On May 28, 1970, the National League of POW/MIA Families was formed with the mission to:

- obtain the release of all prisoners;
- account to the fullest extent possible for missing personnel, and
- repatriate all recoverable remains of those who died serving our nation during the Vietnam War.

This organization became a vital source of clear, timely, and credible information without the bureaucratic screening commonly

Chapter 11

done by the Department of Defense (if and when the DOD decided to communicate at all).

In February of 1971, a former VC stated that he observed a U.S. POW with a gunshot leg wound in a stretcher about 1000 meters from the location where Don went MIA. This source said the POW had been carried there following an engagement between the 31st Regiment, 2nd NVA Division, and troops of the 196th Bde, Americal Division. He identified a picture of Don Sparks as the POW he had seen. This information was received by the Commanding General of the Americal Division in March of 1971.

In November of 1971 a former NVA soldier who was assigned to the 8th BN, 31st Regiment, 2nd NVA Division said he saw a U.S. POW who was wounded in the thigh and evacuated to the 31st Headquarters. These separate, supporting reports were both from Quang Nam Province. Neither were revealed to Don's family for over 20 years.

In 1971, as the rate of U.S. troop withdrawal accelerated, the Sparks experienced increased anxiety. Would the reduced American presence lessen the chances for resolving Don's case? On-the-ground American involvement was winding down and the Christmas 1972 bombing of North Vietnam brought renewed negotiations. On January 27, 1973, Henry Kissinger agreed to a ceasefire that included the repatriation of nearly 600 POWs within 60 days. Between February 12 and March 29, 1973, 591 men were released. The majority were released in Hanoi. Sixty nine were released in South Vietnam. Three were released in China. All were flown in U.S. aircraft to Clark Air Base in the Philippines. Don's Brother Ron was on active duty in the Air Force and stationed in the Philippines at the time of repatriation. Ron would have been nearby if Don had unexpectedly appeared. Sadly, that didn't happen.

At 6:30 a.m. on January 28, 1973. Survivor Assistance Officer Major Keith F. Vansant informed Don's parents that their son was not listed with the POW names presented at the Paris Negotiations. This was followed up with a letter dated January 29, 1973. This communication seems to be one of the few delivered in an appropriate way and in a timely manner.

Imagine being the parent of a son who was not accounted for and hearing the President of the United States assert that all POWs had been returned. That prompted Calvin to write a letter to Richard Nixon, President of the United States stating in part:

> *It is quite shocking when in your T.V. speeches you state all the POWs have returned when your own defense department carries 53 men still as POWs which includes our Son Donald.*
> *I would like a reply including what is being done.*
> *I am sure if it were your son this matter would receive some special attention.*

The letter was received December 3, 1973. Calvin received a response from the Major General of the Army with a stamped, printed signature. It said in part:

> *We are keenly aware of the emotional strain imposed on the families of our captured service men. I trust that your strength and fortitude will sustain you during this trying period of uncertainty.*

This letter arrived eight months after April 1973 when the returning POWs Hal Kushner and Jose Anzaldua had been debriefed and indicated that an American GI by the name of "Don" would be joining them at Jungle Camp. Although this was the best available information about Don's possible whereabouts, the information was not declassified until five years later. Even then, this "additional information was not passed on without delay" to the Sparks family.[36]

By this time, Calvin and Arloha were becoming increasingly concerned about lack of official communication of information. As Captain Kenneth A. Bray Survivor Assistance Officer stated in his July 1978 Report:

> *I went to meet the Sparks family for the first time.*
> *Mother, father, sister, and brother-in-law were present. All*

---

36 To the Army's credit, as Don became eligible for promotions, he was advanced in rank, eventually being promoted to Sergeant First Class. His family received his paychecks on schedule.

were very pleasant and still maintain some hope that SSG Sparks is alive somewhere. Mr. and Mrs. Sparks desire that I visit them quarterly with phone calls during the months I don't visit. This is apparently the relationship they had with previous assistance officers. The only concern the Sparks have is that any information they receive comes from the League of Families or the local American Legion instead of the U.S. Government. They feel that possibly the Government is not as concerned as it once was.

In 1979, the Department of Defense was ready to move forward to change the status of MIAs. In anticipation of this, Calvin submitted a Freedom of Information Act request on September 28, 1978. The response to this request arrived on November 16, 1978 with no mentioned of the declassified POW debriefings.

The family was accorded a hearing on April 19,1979 to state their case against a declaration of death. Ann Mills Griffith from the League of Families of POWs & MIAs was well experienced with these proceedings and was willing to represent the family. Arloha, Esta and Esta's husband, Ervin Behrens, attended along with Ann. During the hearing, Esta opened a folder she had been handed and found a picture of Don she had not seen before. When she asked where the photo came from, they responded, "Where do you think it comes from?" and asked Esta to hand over the folder. She refused until the officials gave the family a copy of the picture. When Esta showed me the picture, I felt confident it was Don's Basic Training identification picture taken after his hair was cut. Why anyone would play games with the picture at the hearing is hard to imagine.

The hearing was merely a formality. A quote from the documented hearing states "Further, the debriefing of returned prisoners of war following the ceasefire agreement of 27 January 1973 has revealed no information of his fate." Don was declared deceased November 5, 1979, a few months more than 10 years after he was captured.

Technically, the argument can be made that Kushner/Anzaldua statements don't indicate what Don's fate was, but it is certainly very relevant information the family should have known at this crucial time. It is not known if this omission was deliberate or a poor service response to a legitimate freedom of information request. In any case, the family did not have and were not provided access to this very relevant POW debriefing information that had been known for six years and unclassified for eight months.

The conduct of the hearing did not leave a good feeling with the Sparks family as indicated in the report filed by Captain Kenneth A. Bray, Survivor Assistance Officer:

> *On 15 May 1979, I brought Maj. Robert Devens, the new SAO, to the Sparks family. Mr. and Mrs. Sparks and their son Russell were present. They were very cordial; however, Mrs. Sparks felt she was treated poorly by officers at DA when she attended the casualty status hearing on 19 April 1979. She said she was treated very "coldly" and that apparently upset her some. The family continues to feel that the League of Families works harder and cares more about her son than DA does.*

The 1979 hearing was a turning point for the family's trust in the government as a source of information regarding Don. In 1989, Calvin said, following the hearing in Washington, he had little to do with official government agencies. He preferred to work with the National League of Families of POW/MIAs.

Clearly, the favorable perception that LTC Batt had fostered in 1970 had waned, not because of a single incident, but through an accumulation of multiple interactions over the years. The mishandling of Don's letters, the lack of contact for long periods, and the failure to reveal relevant information (either deliberately or inadvertently) had taken a huge toll. Add to that, the rude behavior at the April 19, 1979, hearing and it is a wonder the family still has any respect for the U.S. Army.

In November 13, 1982, the Vietnam Veterans Memorial Wall was dedicated. After the original controversy over its design subsided, most people have come to regard it as an appropriate tribute to those who lost their lives in a very divisive war. Don's name was among the 58,318 names enshrined in the nation's capital as a grim reminder of the high cost in lives between 1959 and 1975.

In December of 1987, Arloha passed away. She never gave up hope that Don would return home. A 1985 quote best describes her steadfast faith in a positive outcome: "We never give up hope. You just go from day to day and just hope and pray that he will come home. If you give up hope, you give up everything. We believe he is alive over there." In September 1992, Calvin passed away.

The Defense Authorization Act of 1992/1993 included a SEC. 1082. DISCLOSURE OF INFORMATION CONCERNING UNITED STATES PERSONNEL CLASSIFIED AS PRISONER OF WAR OR MISSING IN ACTION DURING VIETNAM CONFLICT. As the title implies, it required the Department of Defense to release to families information regarding their loved ones. It is hard to believe that an Act of Congress was required to provide information that would alleviate families' anxieties about the fate of loved ones. Yet, clearly this was necessary for Don's family.

In fact, the Sparks family would not become aware of the information obtained from the Kushner/Anzaldua debriefings for another thirteen years after declassification. Don's case narrative was prepared to present to the Vietnamese Government at a Technical Meeting on December 10 and 11, 1992. That Case Narrative included the guards' and English interpreters' references to a POW named "Don" who did not arrive at Jungle Camp as scheduled. The English version of the case narrative was mailed with a cover letter to Mr. and Mrs. Calvin Sparks at their rural Carroll, Iowa, address on February 4, 1993. Apparently the Army did not know that Arloha and Calvin had already passed away. Almost 20 years after the government first obtained the information from the returning POWs in 1973, it was incidentally disclosed to the Sparks family in a document prepared to discuss their son with the Vietnamese.

Don's older brother Ron became the primary contact with the Defense Department after Calvin passed. He was soon confronted by another strange twist in the family's story. A woman named Elaine appeared at a Family Conference claiming to be Don's half-sister. An older relative had told her Calvin was her father, a claim Ron knew to be preposterous. As he described in a letter to the Department of Defense, his parents were never separated during the time Elaine would have been conceived. Ron asked Elaine to present proof in the form of letters, pictures, or anything else she might have. She indicated she would do that the next day. She did not show up. Obviously, this was another incident causing unnecessary grief to a family already coping with an extremely trying situation. Her initial contact with the Department of Defense requesting information was in April of 1993. She followed up with a Freedom of Information Act request in 1997. She has not been heard from since then.

On July 11, 1995 relations with Vietnam were normalized and resolution of individual POW/MIA cases could be formalized. Don's case was recognized as a Last Known Alive (LKA) Case which gave it highest priority for attempted resolution.

In July of 2000, Don's sister, Esta Raasch (formerly Behrens) joined her brother Ron as a recipient of information regarding Don's case. She has now transitioned into the primary family contact person with the Department of Defense. In 2000, she started receiving Family Conference documents providing information on Don's case. The last one containing any new information appeared in 2011. In the past, the Department of Defense has never informed the family of any investigative work on Don's case. Consequently, it is not known if any additional work is now underway or planned. Currently, the Defense POW/MIA Accounting Agency (DPAA) is the branch of the Department of Defense responsible for investigation of cases. After a period of disarray and inadequate funding, the branch has recently gained renewed hope under long-awaited new leadership.

As disappointing as communication with the Department of Defense has been through the years, the fact remains, they are the agency that must be dealt with to resolve Don's case. The individuals responsible for the past are no longer involved. The future depends on those currently in positions of responsibility who are given the financial resources and authority to achieve the fullest possible accounting of POW/MIA cases.

Calvin and Arloha Sparks are buried in Glidden where the family holds a spot for Don's remains to be laid to rest. While there is no longer any expectation that Don is alive, there is still hope that his remains will be recovered. However, time is of the essence. The acidic soils and tropical climate make remains deteriorate faster than in temperate climates. Also, the number of people who might remember key information about Don's burial site is rapidly decreasing. While several

Chapter 11

people who were in Tien Lanh Village area during the 1969-1970 era have been interviewed, we are not aware that anyone in the Thon bon Hamlet south area has been interviewed. Relatively few people were there at the time and even fewer are still living. Interviewing them is very time sensitive.

As of January 19, 2019, there are 1,590 unresolved Vietnam POW/MIA cases in southeast Asia. Of these, 1,247 are located in Vietnam, with 795 cases specifically identified as located in the area formerly known as South Vietnam.[37]

Among the MIA/POW cases, 196 were specially designated as Last Known Alive (LKA). These were given highest priority for resolution.

Of the 196 cases, 176 have been confirmed as deceased, but in only 51 cases have the remains actually been located and confirmed. Efforts continue to locate the remaining 125 who are known to be dead.

Twenty of the 196 cases remain unresolved with no information confirming death or location of the remains. Don Sparks is one of those remaining 20 cases. His status remains

LAST KNOWN ALIVE.

---

[37] The exact number of soldiers classified as POW/MIA changes periodically as cases are resolved.

EPILOGUE

REMEMBERING DON SPARKS

THE SPARKS' FAMILY HAS NOT YET HAD THE SOLACE of a funeral for Don. Had such a ceremony been possible, Don's friend Jim Wiederin might have shared the following memories from their carefree days.[38]

> *I believe we met when we started going to school in Glidden for our 6th grade year, he from Carrollton and me from Ralston. We were both 'good ole farm boys' and each seemed to have a knack of being full of mischief but never getting in big trouble. Just kept the pot stirred up. I kinda remember Don being involved in locking Mr. Mays (a teacher) in the storage room across from the lunchroom in the school. We were in quite a few of the same classes through the rest of our time at GR and got to be best buds. I was not too far away from Don when he lost the tip of his little finger on the grinder during Shop class. He let out a scream that brought everyone running. We were Future*

---

38 These memories were shared with me in an email Jim Wiederin sent me 2-25-2016.

Farmers of America (FFA) officers during our senior year. Seems like we were together 'several' times for evening school activities and then the 'post activity' horsing around. Somebody had to keep Benny (the law) on his toes! Our little group relocated the Glidden police car from in front of the City Hall to the snow drift on the football field. It was just a prank then....now they would call it GTA (grand theft auto). We got stopped by a state trooper one summer evening on our way to the town celebration in Dedham or Willey for some Buds, somebody said you had to be 21?????

Don asked me to take him to the Des Moines airport... guessing in 1968? I believe he was going overseas for a course while attending ISU. This should have been a pretty uneventful outing! Somehow there was a SNAFU with timing and/or meeting location. I will always blame Don... he seemed to always be on his own schedule and seldom in a hurry to get where he was going. I remember meeting or passing Homer (locally known snail's pace driver) at least 3 times while Kathy and I flew between Carroll and Glidden trying to catch up with Don. Not sure how we got to the airplane before it departed. Glad that '65 Super Sport ran pretty good. Don and I were as close as brothers....tons of fond memories! I can still see that green '54 Chevy cruising up and down the streets.

Just thought of something...maybe we're drawn together to be buddies by each other's 'flat-top' hair styles.

The Glidden Graphic (sure is difficult to type with tears running outa my eyes!) had our pictures in the same issue.....Don's MIA/POW (6/17/69) and our wedding article (6/14/69). Kathy and I used to 'go back home' every 3-4 weeks to visit our families. Often times I thought I would make a little side trip to visit Don's parents...sorry I could never muster the courage...I have since wished countless times I would have!

Hey Perkey, Hope you don't mind the rambling on that I included since it does not pertain to the party...just fond

memories about a near and dear friend! Still have the POW bracelet on my wrist.
   Best of luck!!! Good chatting w/ you....Wied

HONORING DON SPARKS

It was a warm summer evening in 1966 when 11-year-old Cathie Betts Fowler faced her fear of riding the Tilt-A-Wheel. She was at the Glidden, Iowa, street-fair with her twin sister, Connie Betts Mills, and their friend Esta Sparks under the supervision of Esta's big brother, Donald. Don, who was home from break from Iowa State, eased Cathie's trepidation by offering to go on the ride with her. "I just remember he was so nice," said Fowler. "When you're a sixth-grader and look up to this college boy, you get a little crush, at least for the evening." That night no one imagined Don would face an enemy ambush in Vietnam three years later.

All these years later, Cathie has established the Donald L. Sparks Gold Star Memorial Scholarship for Iowa State students from Carroll County studying agriculture related fields. Along with the scholarship funds, student recipients will receive the story of Don's life and service to his country. "I want his sacrifice in Vietnam to never be forgotten" said Fowler of her former Tilt-A-Wheel companion. "I want future generations to walk through the Gold Star Hall and think of him. If they see his name on the wall and they have the scholarship in his name, his legacy will live on."

For more information about the scholarship, contact:

Iowa State University Foundation
2505 University Boulevard
P.O. Box 2230
Ames, Iowa 50010-2230
Toll-free: 800-621-8515
wwwIsugift.org

KEEPING FAITH

My family has had a huge range of emotions from experiencing a sibling and son being injured in basic training but yet sent to Vietnam and wounded and captured to an array of fellowships and support to seeing the pain and anguish in our parent's lives day after day; year after year.

Don had a great education from Glidden-Ralston Community School and Iowa State University and was so blessed to complete his studies before being drafted and sent to Vietnam.

We have worked with a number of casualty officers. Some we found to be compassionate and willing to go the extra step to help in any way. Working with The League of POW & MIA Families has been very helpful; they are very caring to the point of having the director serving as Power of Attorney at Don's status hearing.

We still attend Family Update Meetings throughout the United States. We have grown to know that Don may not come home alive. Nevertheless, finding and bringing Don home will always be our mission. I will always have that hope and faith to believe he will come home. The search is on-going, not only for Don but for all POWs who have not returned as well as those who are MIA. Don is on the "Last Known Alive" list and his file is brought to their attention with each visit that the Defense POW/MIA Accounting Agency makes to Vietnam.

Through all this tragedy I have grown to know and become close to a lot of Don's friends from high school and college. What a great group of guys who have reached out to me and formed brother and sister ties. With each one telling me their stories of Don and with each one's personality, a little of Don's character and personality is brought back to me: serious, dedicated, fun loving, quiet, teasing, joking, hard working. All parts and pieces that I treasure. What a great feeling to know that each one of them was a super friend of Don's and miss him as much as I do.

An old friend of mine from my 4-H days thought so much of Don for his kind gestures that she honored him by establishing the Donald L. Sparks Gold Star Memorial Scholarship.

Wonderful people—all part of Don's past—now make up my huge family. I will always treasure their friendships!

I want to especially thank Arlyn Perkey for putting Don's life into this book. I am so grateful for all the dedication and hard work he has done. All the information he has obtained has enlightened me. His expertise in communicating with fellow grunts has really helped to make sense of all the events that happened. He explains them in ways that help you feel you are right at the scene of the event.

I wish to thank all military personnel for their service to this fine nation. God bless them with huge hugs of welcome home. May all families of POWs and MIAs find peace and comfort.

UNTIL WE MEET AGAIN

I have been asked, "How do you feel now?" I interpret this to mean, "After all the document digging and phone conversations, do you feel better than you did?" The short answer is "yes, much better." The longer answer is a mixed bag as life usually is. Obviously, from the tone of my writing, there have been disappointments; things that I wish would have been handled differently. Most people who look back with reasonable objectivity see things they would do differently if they had the chance. I know I do. However, there are no do-overs. It was what it was. Our only real option is what to do now.

I choose to treasure every phone conversation with every individual. They all helped me gain insight into what happened. I hope we helped each other. Don would want that for us.

The question "How do I feel now?" suggests the task is done. It isn't. When I sign on to the Virtual Wall and enter the name Donald L. Sparks, I want a correct account of his ordeal and fate to appear. With the help of the Sparks family, I want that message to accurately reflect what happened to Don.

When Don's remains are recovered and returned for burial beside his parents in Glidden, Iowa, I want to give Esta a hug, and say "Now we have done the best we could do for him."

Then, when I get my final call and see Don in heaven, I want to start the conversation something like this: "Freshman English at Iowa State was tough, but life got tougher after that. Tell me, Donny, when you said, 'Now I have myself ready' before going to Vietnam, were you really ready for what happened?" Then I will see that ornery grin appear on his face, and he will tell me the rest of the story. Then the task will be done. Then we can both rest in peace.

ACKNOWLEDGMENTS

Thank you to the Sparks Family, especially Don's sister Esta Raasch for trusting me to tell Don's story, and then working with me as we plodded forward putting the pieces of the puzzle together. At times I am sure it seemed like there was never any good news, only more anguish as we learned more details. Your patience, perseverance, and flexibility are greatly appreciated.

Thank you to my wife Marial for the willingness to tolerate my venting, preoccupation, and at times almost obsession with the pursuit. Without my editor, Maria Piantanida, you wouldn't be able to make sense of this. Beyond the grammar and organization, I needed those "what about this? – you already said that, and a few – better left unsaids." Thank you, Patrick L. Hoover for your help with the photos and book cover. Your patience with us is admirable.

A huge thank you to all the men from Don's company, C Co., 3/21st, 196th LIB, Americal Division who were willing to share what they knew: Joel Pasternack, James Gordon, Marvin Timperley, Al Shaw, Fred Salerno, Jim "Doc" McCloughan, Tom Pozdol, John Guccione, August Weidner, David Classick, Dennis O'Neill, and Charles Miller. At times it was not easy to open those memories. I also know what I told you was not easy to hear. The Charlie Tigers (C Company) web site, maintained by Earl Powers was used extensively. The only picture of Don Sparks in Vietnam that the family has came from the "Unknown Men" page of the web site. The family and I thank all of you. Priscilla Graham, Larry Graham's niece, graciously shared the photos of Larry taken before he was KIA.

When Gary Borkowski, Jerry Reeves, and Marcel Gorre from my company, D Co., 1st BN/8th Cav., 1st Air Cavalry, shared their memories, it gave me additional perspectives and made me aware that two people in the same place at the same time with adrenalin pumping, may remember things differently. From my D company, I relied on the WeBeWebbiers internet site maintained by Gordon Swenson. The diary from Ed Nored is the basis for much of the information we have of that 1-year time period. I appreciate being able to use photos from the site.

I don't know who from the 1st Platoon, 5 th/46 th, 196th LIB, Americal Division to thank for recovering Don's two letters. Without them and Dave Krommenhoek, I don't know when, if ever, we would have learned Don was a POW. Authors David W. Taylor and Ken Teglia were very helpful in providing what they knew about that portion of Don's story. Joe Scurlock, the medic with C company, 5th/46th gave us the description of the Hospital as it was in August of 1968.

Thank you to John Ealy for putting me in touch with Esta to get this endeavor started. Ellis Macha, Jim and Clay Brinker, Jim Wiederin, and Cathie Betts Fowler all shared beautiful memories of the Don we knew and loved.

I am also grateful to the post-war interviewers and support staff and the Vietnamese personnel who shared memories. Without investigations conducted by the Defense POW/MIA Accounting Agency we wouldn't know much about Don's post-capture experience. Finally, thank you to whoever should be credited for the 1992/1993 Defense Authorization Act which provided for Section 1082, Disclosure of Information Concerning United States Personnel Classified as Prisoner of War or Missing in Action during Vietnam Conflict. Without this requirement to release information to the families, it is doubtful we would know as much as we do.

APPENDIX 1

Timeline of Events

CHAPTERS ARE ARRANGED TO CONTRIBUTE to the reader's understanding of Donald Lee Sparks being drafted into the United States Army, placed in the infantry, sent to Vietnam, captured by the NVA, and held captive as a POW. Events using Arlyn's (the author's) experience in Vietnam are not necessarily in chronological order nor are they in sequence with when Don would have had a somewhat similar experience.

The following timeline with events in chronological order is provided to help guide the reader who may want to be familiar with the sequence of events for Don and Arlyn. The center column indicates the date when an event occurred. Bolded text indicates events of primary significance. Unbolded text indicates relevant background information.

For example, of primary significance, in June 1968, Don went on a European Tour to earn credits toward graduating from Iowa State University. During that same time period, Arlyn started work on the White Mountain National Forest in New Hampshire.

DON	TIME	ARLYN
	May 1968	Graduate from Iowa State University
European Agriculture Tour of 12 countries	June 1968	Work on White Mountain NF in New Hampshire
Graduate from Iowa State University	August 1968	
On Farm in Iowa	October 16, 1968	**Drafted into Army**
Drafted into Army	December 1968	Basic Training – Ft. Polk
Basic Training-Ft. Ord, CA	January 1969	Advanced Infantry Training Ft. Polk, LA
Advanced Infantry Training Ft. Ord, CA	March 1969	NCO School - Ft. Benning, GA
Don leaves IA for VN	April 24, 1969	

Don arrives VN	May 12, 1969	
C 3/21st suffers heavy losses, 1 POW	May 13, 14, 15, 1969	
With C 3/21st Americal Div. in the bush	May 30, 1969	Drops out NCO school
WIA & captured	June 17, 1969	Iowa on pre-Vietnam leave
Family notified MIA	June 20, 1969	Leave IA for Vietnam
Bn. Commander visits C Co. night laager location	June 21, 1969	Report to Presidio in CA
Board of Inquiry at LZ Center regarding MIA	June 26, 1969	
At or near CK 120 hospital	July 4, 1969	**Arrive in Vietnam**
Gn. Westmoreland's MIA letter to Don's parents	July 5, 1969	
Rescue of C 3/21st POW, Larry Aiken from CK 130	July 10, 1969	
CK 120 Hospital	July 20, 1969	With D, 1st 8th Cav., 1st Air Cav. In the bush
Larry Aiken dies from wounds suffered July 10	July 25, 1969	Cherry In The Bush
Letter to Don's parents purporting MIA event	August 8, 1969	Carrying M-60 machine gun
Jim Gordon visits ambush site & finds only craters	August 29-31, 1969	
CIDG report American seen east of CK 120	September 18, 1969	
	September 28, 1969	**Chuck Deaton KIA, An Eye For An Eye**
Walking with quasi crutch, made escape attempts	December 9, 1969	**WIA, gunshot in left arm**
	December 23, 1969	**Arrive at home in Iowa**
Moved from CK 120 H. "Into The Mountains"	February 10, 1970	Surgery on arm at Fitzsimmons Hospital
Writes 2 Letters Home, from the Mountains	April 11, 1970	
	April 30, 1970	**Watch Nixon announce Cambodian incursion**
Letters purporting Don was KIA filed at C Co.	May 12, 1970	

Appendix 1

VC political officer killed; Don's letters recovered; Krommenhoek writes letter	May 17, 1970	
1st Platoon Leader Mower, KIA (letter recovery)	May 21, 1970	
Joint Personnel Recovery Center provided letters	May 22, 1970	
Examiner states Don is "probable" author	May 26, 1970	
The National League of POW/MIA Families formed	May 28, 1970	
Mrs. Kaufmann writes letter to Mayor, Carroll, IA; Sheriff contacts family	June 5, 1970	
Calvin Sparks writes Dave Krommenhoek	June 12, 1970	
Calvin asks LTC Batt for help to get Don's letters	June 17, 1970	
Calvin notes receipt of "To Everyone At Home" letter	August 10, 1970	
	October 6, 1970	**Discharged from Army**
	October 25, 1970	**Report, White Mountain NF, Gorham, NH**
Expert confirmation of authenticity Don's letters	November 25, 1970	
Don's status changed from MIA to captured	December 1, 1970	
LTC Batt delivers Don's DM letter to Calvin & Arloha	January 1971	
Ex-VC identifies Don's picture as POW with leg gunshot wound	February 1971	
Ex NVA reports seeing wounded US POW Quan Nam Province	November 1971	
Few U.S. ground combat troops still in Vietnam	June 10, 1972	**Married (first time)**

Intense bombing of North Vietnam	Christmas 1972	
Cease fire & agreement to release POWs	January 27, 1973	Saco RD, White Mountain NF, Conway, NH
Family notified that Don not on POW release list	January 28, 1973	
591 POW's released	February 12-March 29, 1973	
POW's Kushner & Anzaldua debriefed; tell of POW, "Don"	April 1973	
Former PAVN medic reports seeing American POW with long nose	October 1973	
	November 1974	**Daughter Karen born**
Saigon Falls – the Vietnam War is over, for some	April 30, 1975	Saco RD, White Mountain NF, Conway, NH
	October 1976	**Son David born**
1973 POW debriefings declassified	August 27, 1978	Hoosier NF, Bedford, IN
Calvin submits Freedom Of Information Act request	September 28, 1978	
Calvin receives response to FOIA request	November 16, 1978	
Hearing on Don's MIA/POW status	April 19, 1979	Deer River RD, Chippewa NF, MN
Don is declared deceased	November 5, 1979	
	May 1980	**NA, S&PF, US Forest Service, Portsmouth, NH**
	November 1981	**Read 10,000 Day War**
Don's name on Vietnam Memorial, Washington DC	November 1982	
	August 1983	**NA, S&PF, US Forest Service, Morgantown, WV**
	October 1983	**Read History of the Vietnam War**

Appendix 1

	November 1983	Learned Don is POW
Arloha Sparks passes away	December 1987	
Interview Vietnamese who saw Don after capture	April 1989	
Former CK120 Hospital staff interviewed	August 1990	
	April 1991	Divorced 1st wife
POW/MIA disclosure provision in Defense Authorization Act	March 1, 1992	
Calvin Sparks passes away	September 1992	
Ron Sparks becomes family contact with DOD	September 1992	
Don's Case summary presented to VN gov't	December 10 & 11, 1992	
Former CK120 Hospital staff interviewed	January 1993	
Investigate potential burial site in mountains	August 1994	
Relations with Vietnam normalized	July 11, 1995	
	May 20, 2000	Married 2nd wife, Marial
Esta Raasch begins transition to primary family contact with DOD	July 2000	
CK 120 staff interviewed	November 2000	
Interview CK120 medic & food provider	June 2010	
Interview more CK120 staff & NVA who saw Don	March/April 2011	
Interview political officer who captured Don 1st time	May 2011	
Interview NVA political officer who saw Don	May 2012	
Don honored at 50th high school reunion	August 2014	
	September 27, 2014	50th High School Class Reunion

Esta gives consent to reach out to Don's Co.	October 2014	Talk to Esta about contact with Don's company
Don added to Iowa State University Gold Star Hall	November 11, 2014	
Esta sends case files to assist with contact info	March 2, 2015	
Don Sparks Gold Star Scholarship established	October 2017	**Start writing book**
1st Scholarship recipient receives funds	January 2019	
	April 2019	**Ready to publish book**
50 Years after Capture	June 17, 2019	

APPENDIX 2A

*Chain of Command Chart for Arlyn Perkey
(9-28-1969)*

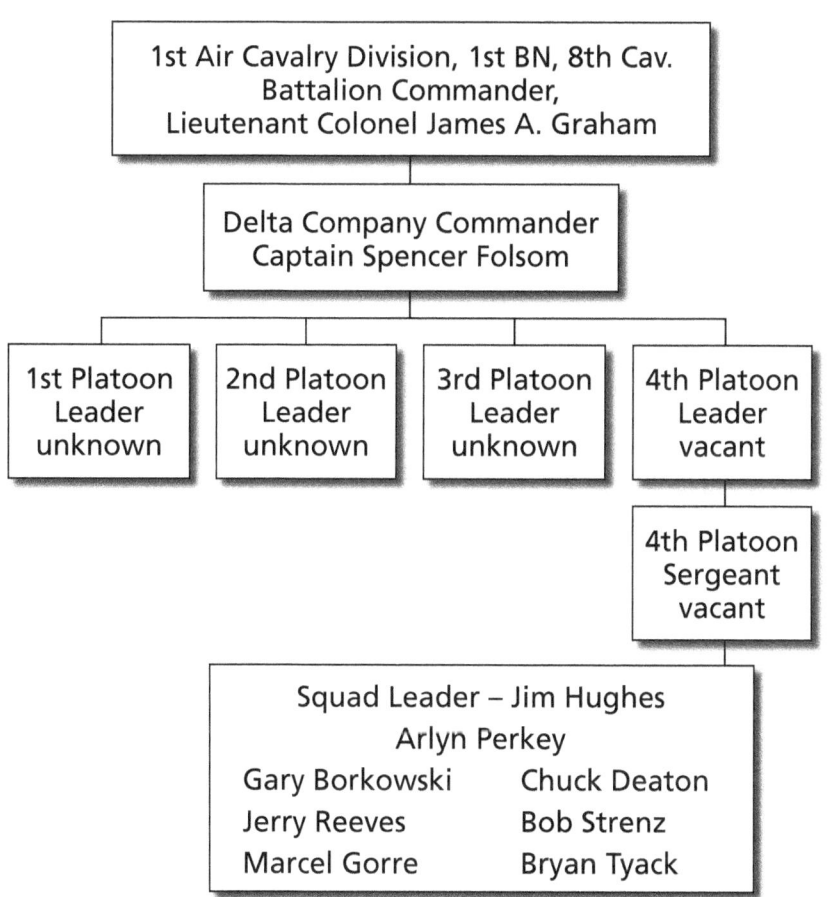

APPENDIX 2B

Chain of Command Chart for Arlyn Perkey (12-9-1969)

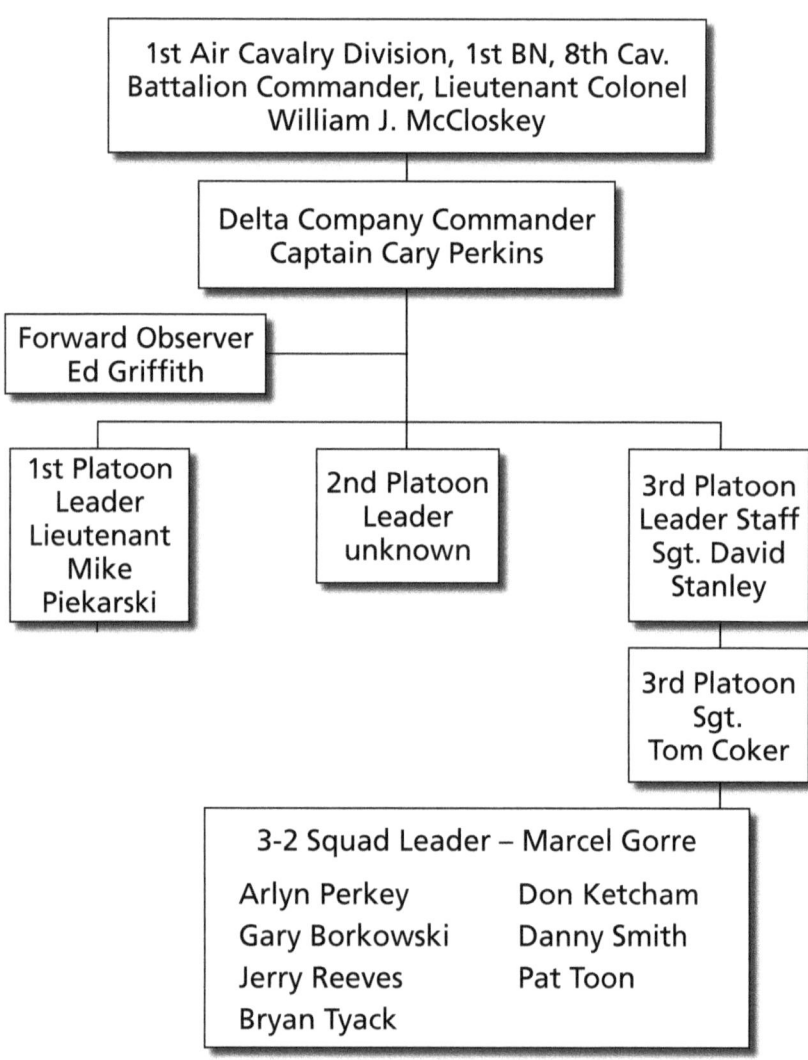

APPENDIX 2C

Chain of Command for Donald L Sparks (6-17-1969)

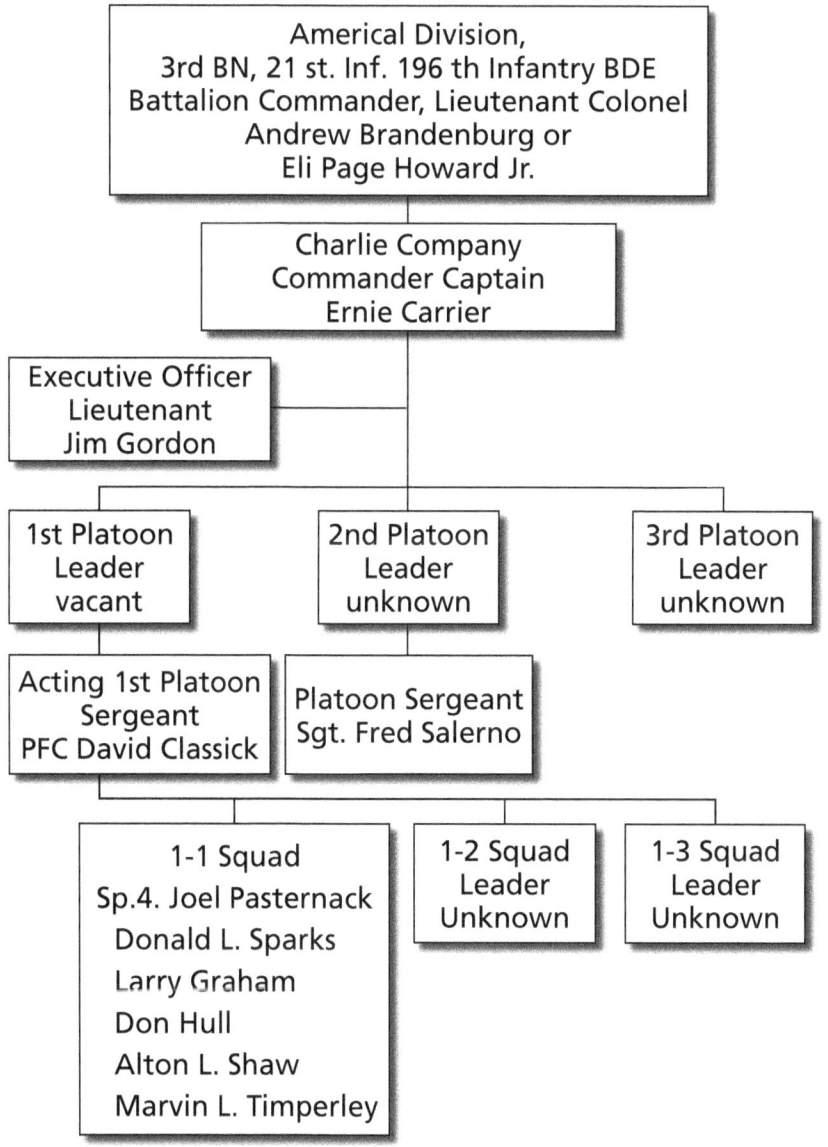

APPENDIX 3
Key Military Grid Locations

THE SKETCH MAPS USED IN THIS TEXT are derived from the military grid locations taken from The Duty Officer's Log and applied to 1:50,000 topographic maps developed by the Defense Mapping Agency in the late 1960's and early 1970's. In 1969, Company Commanders were often using an earlier version of these maps to identify on-the-ground locations. Accuracy of locations varied depending on who was assessing the terrain and the landmarks they had available to make the determination. If the following locations are used on Google Earth with the Military Grid option, significant variation from the map location may be observed. Google Earth shows 5 digits easterly and northerly while the most common level of precision on the Duty Officers Log was 3 digits easterly and northerly. In 50 years, there have been significant changes in road locations and land use. Many areas that were jungle in 1969, have been altered to agricultural and other uses. Maps are available from the United States Geological Survey.

Appendix 3

Key Military Grid Locations for Don Sparks in Vietnam

KEY LOCATION	MILITARY GRID 49P	MAP NAME & NUMBER
		Series L7014
LZ Center	BT 050 252	TAM KY (WEST) 6640 II
Don's capture 6-17-1969	BT 099 234	TAM KY (WEST) 6640 II
C company night location	BT 095 225	TAM KY (WEST) 6640 II
6:10 am 6-17-1969 incident	BT 100 234	TAM KY (WEST) 6640 II
Evening 6-17-69 sighting	BT 085 235	TAM KY (WEST) 6640 II
Aide Station	BT 08 24	TAM KY (WEST) 6640 II
Tien Ha sighting	BT 028 206	HIEP DUC 6640 III
NVA 31st Regimental HDQT	BT 005 225	HIEP DUC 6640 III
CIDG sighting	BT 014 099	HAU DUC 6639 IV
CIDG sighting	BT 015 074	HAU DUC 6639 IV
Hospital CK 120	AT 96 10 & AT 96 11	HAU DUC 6639 IV
Cau Chim Crossroads	AT 975 975	HAU DUC 6639 IV
Jungle Camp	AT 91 05	HAU DUC 6639 IV
Hanoi Mountain	AT 89 05	HAU DUC 6639 IV
Thon bon 13	AT 888 014	HAU DUC 6639 IV
Letters Recovered	BT 351 045	LY TIN 6739 IV

Key Military Grid Locations for Arlyn Perkey in Vietnam

KEY LOCATION	MILITARY GRID 48P	MAP NAME & NUMBER
LZ Ellen	YU 035 064	PHUOC BINH 6332 I
LZ JERRI	XU 963 235	PHUOC BINH 6332 I
Deaton KIA	XU 905 159	PHUOC BINH 6332 I
McRight/Haushultz KIA	XU 928 128	PHUOC BINH 6332 I
Miller KIA	XU 918 128	PHUOC BINH 6332 I
12-9-1969 Ambush	XU 916 134	PHUOC BINH 6332 I

Learning Moments Press is an independent publishing company dedicated to sharing the wisdom that comes from thoughtful reflection on experience. The Wisdom of Life Series offers insightful reflections on significant life events that challenge the meaning of one's life, one's sense of self, and one's place in the world.

Cooligraphy artist Daniel Nie created the logo for Learning Moments Press by combining two symbol systems. Following the principles of ancient Asian symbols, Daniel framed the logo with the initials of Learning Moments Press. Within this frame, he has replicated the Adinkra symbol for Sankofa as interpreted by graphic artists at the Documents and Design Company. As explained by Wikipedia, Adinkra is a writing system of the Akan culture of West Africa. Sankofa symbolizes taking from the past what is good and bringing it into the present in order to make positive progress through the benevolent use of knowledge. Inherent in this philosophy is the belief that the past illuminates the present and that the search for knowledge is a life-long process.

www.ingramcontent.com/pod-product-compliance
Lightning Source LLC
Chambersburg PA
CBHW051600010526
44118CB00023B/2759